TIFFY CHEN started blogging about food and recipes after learning how to cook from her mother and grandmother. In her debut cookbook, Tiffy shares memories and recipes shaped by growing up in Taiwan—a country with a rich culture, diverse cuisines, and some of the best street food in the world—along with beloved family recipes and unique dishes inspired by her travels across Southeast Asia.

With 88 (a very lucky number in Chinese culture) flavor-packed recipes, Tiffy offers her favorite quick-and-easy everyday dishes, like a classic **Taiwanese Breakfast Sandwich** and her grandmother's **Sesame Chicken Rice**. Also included are family-style dishes to pass around and enjoy, from **Drunken Chicken** and **Braised Five-Spice Beef** to **Garlic and Scallion Lobster** and **Braised Sticky Pork Belly**. You'll find favorites like bao, buns, wontons, and dumplings that are great to make in bulk—all freezer-friendly to help you save time and have them on hand for when the mood strikes!

With gorgeous step-by-step photography and heartwarming stories about traveling in Asia and finding the best street food in Taiwan, *Tiffy Cooks* celebrates Asian food and family in this must-make collection of go-to recipes.

TIFFY
COOKS

**88 Easy Asian Recipes
from My Family to Yours**

TIFFY CHEN

TEN SPEED PRESS
California | New York

This book is dedicated to my family, as it is
a culmination of all our stories and memories.

Contents

Recipes

traveled to helped shape my palate and my love for different cuisines. I believe that all the ups and downs brought me to where I am today.

When I quit my full-time job to pursue being a food blogger full-time, it was scary, but I knew I was ready. As my reach and audience grew, my love for food and what I do grew with it. Never in a million years would I ever have imagined being able to publish a cookbook of my family's recipes and to be able to share it with the world.

Food is our love language, and in these pages are 88 of my recipes that I hope you will use to express your own love.

Basic Tools

- Wok (14-inch carbon steel is ideal)
- Bamboo (or metal) steamer (two or three tiers with a lid)
- Deep-frying thermometer
- Frying pans (medium and large; nonstick is best for egg and crepe recipes)
- Pots (small, medium, and large; deep pot for deep-frying)
- Cheesecloth (for making milk)
- Chopsticks
- Fine-mesh sieve
- Rolling pin
- Spider (mesh skimmer)
- Steamer liner or perforated parchment paper
- Wok spatula
- Clay pot (nice to have, but not essential)
- Sizzling plate (nice to have, but not essential)

My Taiwanese Pantry

Condiments and Spices

One of my favorite things about cooking at home is that you can customize your ingredients to suit your diet and what you are able to source in your area. Here are the condiments and spices that I always keep stocked in my own pantry, along with substitutions you can use depending on any dietary restrictions. The brands that I recommend are not only my go-to brands, but they are also readily available at your local Asian grocery store or online.

GFO = gluten-free option
VO = vegetarian option

Condiments

Soy Sauce (醬油 Jiangyou)

If there is one condiment I cannot live without, it is definitely soy sauce. It is a staple ingredient that I always have in my kitchen. There are many different variations of soy sauce, and depending on the country and cuisine, these can be used in a variety of different dishes. Soy sauce is one of the oldest condiments in the world. In fact, soybeans and wheat were first fermented with brine around 2,500 years ago, during the Western Han dynasty in China. Each soy sauce brand has its own flavor, texture, saltiness, sweetness, and appearance, depending how it was brewed.

In this cookbook, I mainly use *light soy sauce* (not low sodium) and have been specific in the recipes—preferably Chinese or Taiwanese—unless stated otherwise. Note that "light soy sauce" does not refer to low sodium (see recommended brands below). Light soy sauce is saltier and has a thinner consistency than dark soy sauce. It's often used in stir-fries, in dipping sauces, and as a seasoning.

Brands I Like: Wan Ja Shan Vintage Soy Sauce, Lee Kum Kee Premium Soy Sauce
GFO: If you have a gluten allergy, you can use tamari in place of soy sauce.

Dark Soy Sauce (老抽 Lao chou)

Whenever I call for dark soy sauce in a recipe, the most common question I get asked is, "Can I just double the amount of light soy sauce?" The answer is no! Because dark soy sauce is darker, people often assume it's saltier. But it's actually the opposite: dark soy sauce is not as salty as light soy sauce. If you have ever wondered how Taiwanese braised meat gets its beautiful color without over-the-top saltiness, the secret ingredient is dark soy sauce.

Dark soy sauce is a staple kitchen condiment that is essential in Taiwanese cooking. It is perfect for adding color to a dish and for braising without intensifying saltiness. It is sweeter, thicker, and has more depth of flavor than light soy sauce. I recommend adding it to your pantry. A little goes a long way. Unlike light soy sauce, it normally takes me over three months to finish a bottle. Store dark soy sauce in the fridge once opened.

Brands I Like: Lee Kum Kee Premium Dark Soy Sauce

Black Vinegar (烏醋 Wu cu)

Black vinegar is a staple condiment in most Taiwanese pantries. It's the most popular dipping sauce for dumplings, wontons, and pastries. There is a big difference between Taiwanese black vinegar and Chinese black vinegar. Taiwanese black vinegar has a smoky aroma similar to Worcestershire sauce, and it is seasoned with fermented fruits and vegetables, giving it a slightly sweet aftertaste. Like dark soy sauce, a little goes a long way. Store it in the fridge once opened. If you can't find Taiwanese black vinegar, mix ½ part Worcestershire sauce with 1 part rice vinegar and 1 part light soy sauce.

Brands I Like: Kong Yen Black Vinegar (this is the only brand I use)

Rice Vinegar (米醋 Micu)

Rice vinegar is made from fermented rice. Compared to Western white vinegar, it is sweeter and less acidic. I like to use rice vinegar to add acidity to my pickled vegetables. There are many brands on the market, but if you can't find any, you can use sushi seasoning (Mizkan vinegar sushi seasoning) or apple cider vinegar instead.

Brands I Like: Kong Yen Rice Vinegar, Mizkan Rice Vinegar

Sesame Oil (麻油 Mayou)

Just like soy sauce, every Asian country has its own take on sesame oil. There are numerous varieties, depending on how (and whether) the sesame is roasted and how it's pressed. When my recipes call for sesame oil, I mean *toasted* sesame oil. Toasted oil has a deeper, toastier flavor than regular, or light, sesame oil, so it is generally used as a condiment to finish a dish. It also has a low smoking point, so it's rarely used for cooking (unlike regular sesame oil). It's worth noting that sesame oil has a very strong, fragrant smell. Like many of the other condiments listed here, a little goes a long way. If it's your first time using sesame oil, I recommend adding it to a dish a little at a time and tasting as you go.

Brands I Like: Kadoya Pure Sesame Oil (widely available and the only brand I use)

Oyster Sauce (蠔油 Haoyou)

Oyster sauce is made from oyster extract. It has a slight umami taste and is often used as a dipping sauce, as a marinade, and in stir-fries. It has a thick consistency, making it perfect for giving a glossy finish to any braised dishes. Oyster sauce is not fishy at all. It is salty, sweet, and has a slight umami flavor. Make sure not to confuse oyster sauce with hoisin sauce. Even though they are similar in consistency and color, the flavor is completely different.

If you have a seafood allergy, I recommend using a mushroom-based oyster sauce or vegetarian oyster sauce (see below). Since many of my family members have allergies to shellfish, I use vegetarian oyster sauce in most of my dishes.

Brands I Like: Lee Kum Kee Premium Oyster Flavored Sauce
VO: Vegetarian oyster sauce

Vegetarian Oyster Sauce (醬油膏 Jiangyou gao)

Vegetarian oyster sauce, also known as thick soy sauce in Taiwan, is a staple condiment in my kitchen. If you don't want to overstock your pantry, I recommend buying vegetarian oyster sauce rather than regular oyster sauce. It is sweeter and slightly less salty than regular oyster sauce. You can use vegetarian oyster sauce on its own as a dipping sauce, in stir-fries, and in marinades.

Brands I Like: Wan Ja Shan Vegetarian Mushroom Oyster Sauce

Rice Wine (米酒 Mijiu)

Rice wine is a staple ingredient in my pantry. It is used in many Taiwanese dishes to remove the odor of meat and seafood. It contains approximately 20% alcohol and adds sweetness and depth of flavor, even though it doesn't add much flavor of its own. If you are not able to find rice wine, you can substitute dry sherry. If you cannot consume alcohol, swap the rice wine for an equal amount of water.

Brands I Like: Michiu (rice cooking wine)

Japanese Mayo (美乃滋 Meinai zi)

Japanese mayo, also known as Kewpie mayo, is a popular condiment that's often found in Taiwanese pantries. There are three main differences between Western mayonnaise and Japanese mayonnaise. First, unlike most Western mayo, which uses whole eggs, Japanese mayo is made with only egg yolks, giving it a richer flavor and a custard-like texture. It is also slightly sweeter than Western-style mayo as it is made with rice vinegar rather than white vinegar. And lastly, no salt or other seasoning is added aside from MSG, which gives Japanese mayo its famous umami flavor.

Brands I Like: Kewpie Mayonnaise
VO: Kewpie Egg-Free Vegan Mayonnaise

Spicy Fermented Bean Paste (辣豆瓣醬 La doubanjiang)

One of the most flavorful condiments that adds spicy, savory, and garlic flavors is spicy fermented bean paste. The paste is made from fermented soybeans and broad beans, garlic, and chili. It is an essential condiment that adds so much flavor to a dish. It is a crucial component in many dishes and can't be replaced with something else. Store spicy fermented bean paste in the fridge once it has been opened. Since it is fermented, it has a long shelf life.

Brands I Like: Sichuan Pixian Broad Bean Paste

Homemade Chili Oil and Garlic Oil (辣椒油 蒜蓉油)

The last two condiments that you will *always* find in my fridge are my easy-to-make homemade Chili Oil (page 245) and Garlic Oil (page 246). Preparing condiments ahead of time is one of the easiest ways to save time and money, and is also key to preparing restaurant-quality dishes at home.

Spices

Five-Spice Powder (五香粉 Wuxiang fen)

Five-spice powder is an essential spice in any Taiwanese pantry. The ingredients in the mixture and the amount of each particular spice varies depending on the brand, culture, and also personal preference. You can easily make five-spice powder at home by grinding up the toasted spices, or you can purchase it at Asian grocery markets, at many supermarkets, or online.

The most common ingredients in five-spice powder are star anise, fennel seeds, cloves, and cinnamon sticks. The fifth ingredient might be Sichuan peppercorns, black peppercorns, white peppercorns, or dried sand ginger. Personally, I like five-spice powder that contains Sichuan peppercorns, which give it a slight kick.

If you want to make the powder at home, toast all the whole spices, in equal amounts, together in a dry frying pan for 3 to 4 minutes, until fragrant. Let cool, then grind the spices into a fine powder with a spice grinder. Store in an airtight container at room temperature for up to 5 months. (You can adjust the quantity of each spice used in your five-spice powder based on your preference and the brands used.)

Brands I Like: Flying Swallow Five-Spice Powder

Chicken Powder (雞粉 **Ji fen**)

Chicken powder, also known as chicken bouillon powder, is a secret ingredient in my kitchen because it adds so much flavor to a dish. The concentrated powder is made from dehydrated chicken stock and vegetables, fat, salt, and often MSG. MSG gives instant umami flavor, adding lots of depth to any dish. If you don't consume MSG, there are many brands that are MSG-free. If you are vegetarian, you can swap this out for mushroom powder (see below).

Brands I Like: Knorr Chicken Flavored Broth Mix
VO: Mushroom powder

Mushroom Powder (香菇粉 **Xianggu fen**)

Mushroom powder, also known as mushroom bouillon powder, consists of ground dehydrated mushrooms. Mushrooms are packed with umami flavor. Every brand uses different types of mushrooms, but my go-to is a blend of shiitake and porcini mushrooms. Mushroom powder is a great substitute if you are allergic to the seafood that is in dashi powder or are vegetarian and can't consume chicken powder.

You can buy mushroom powder at Asian grocery stores, but making your own is really easy. Toast chopped mushrooms of your choice in a dry frying pan for 3 to 4 minutes, until fragrant and dried. Cool the mushrooms, then grind into a fine powder with a spice grinder. Sift the powder to remove any chunks. Store in an airtight container in the fridge for up to 3 months.

Brands I Like: Lee Kum Kee Mushroom Bouillon Powder

Dashi Powder (柴魚粉 **Chai yufen**)

Dashi powder is my secret ingredient, and you'll see it in many of my recipes. If you are ever looking to add some amazing umami flavor to your dishes, reach for dashi powder! Dashi powder is an instant soup stock made from dried bonito flakes, kelp, salt, sugar, and amino acids. Some brands also include MSG, which gives the stock even more flavor. Dashi powder sometimes comes in individual packets to make single portions of soup. I like to pour the contents of all the packets into an airtight container; that way, I can use whatever amount I need. A little goes a long way with this powder.

Dashi powder is super affordable and easily purchased online. Also available are vegetarian dashi powders, such as kombu dashi powder, which do not contain dried bonito flakes.

Brands I Like: Ajinomoto Hon Dashi
VO: Kombu dashi powder

Flours and Starches

These can all be found at most Asian grocery stores or online. I find that my preferred brands (listed below) are the most trustworthy in terms of authenticity and successfully re-creating the recipes in this cookbook, but you can definitely use other brands.

Rice Flour (在來米粉 **Zai lai mifen**)

Rice flour is a staple in my kitchen, and I always keep plenty on hand. It's so versatile: it's used as a thickener for soups and as an alternative for wheat flour in baked goods, and it's essential when deep-frying.

Brands I Like: Erawan Thai Rice Flour

Glutinous Rice Flour (糯米粉 **Nuomi fen**)

Glutinous rice flour, also known as sweet rice flour, is ground from sweet white rice. Unlike regular rice flour, glutinous rice flour becomes very sticky when heated up, making it perfect for mochi or rice balls.

Brands I Like: Erawan Sweet Sticky Glutinous Rice Flour

Tapioca Starch/Sweet Potato Starch (地瓜粉 **Digua fen**)

Tapioca starch, also known as sweet potato starch, is a slightly sweet starch that is extracted from tapioca, or cassava, root. It is commonly used in Asian desserts and boba pearls because it provides a chewy texture. It is also used to create crispy coatings on meat and tofu. The best part: it's naturally gluten-free and vegan.

Brands I Like: Imperial Taste Sweet Potato Starch (for deep-fried dishes) or Erawan Tapioca Starch Powder (for pastries/desserts)

Mochiko (甜糯米粉 **Tian nuomi fen**)

Mochiko (sweet rice flour) is another type of flour made from glutinous, or sweet white, rice. It's more finely milled than other rice flours and is typically used in desserts such as mochi because it is made from Japanese short-grain rice and provides a chewy texture.

Brands I Like: Koda Farms Blue Star Mochiko Sweet Rice Flour

Cornstarch (玉米澱粉 **Yumi dianfen**)

Cornstarch is an extremely versatile ingredient that is often used as a coating, for batters, and to thicken sauces and soups. It also adds tenderness to baked goods.

Brands I Like: Kingsford's Corn Starch

Other Spices I Often Use

You can easily find all the spices listed below at your local Asian grocery store or online. Store these spices in airtight containers or spice bags. To enhance the flavor of the spices before using them in a recipe, toast each in a dry frying pan for 3 to 4 minutes, until fragrant.

- Sichuan peppercorns
- Star anise
- Bay leaves
- Korean red chili flakes
- Dried Thai or Chinese whole red chilies
- White peppercorns

Vegetarian Substitutions

Feel free to use these vegetarian substitutions for the following common ingredients in any of my recipes.

oyster sauce → vegetarian oyster sauce
dashi powder → kombu dashi powder
chicken powder → mushroom powder
Japanese mayo → vegetarian mayo
ground meat → crumbled tofu or finely chopped shiitake mushrooms

NOTE: Vegetarian recipes in the book feature a so you find them at a glance.

PART

1

Quick and Easy All Day

These are staple recipes that are constantly on rotation in my daily life. They have a very special place in my heart because these are some of the first dishes I learned to make when I first got started in the kitchen. They feature easy-to-find ingredients and are perfect for busy home cooks who want to prepare delicious meals without spending hours in the kitchen. If you are having a hard time deciding what to eat, I hope you can flip through the pages of this section and find something that is perfect for you!

Breakfast

In Taiwan, breakfast is a very big deal. It truly is the most important meal of the day, and it shows in our culture. When you see children walking to school, you'll notice almost every kid has a takeout breakfast in their hand. Most adults commuting to work will stop by their favorite breakfast joint to pick something up before continuing on their way. Everyone is always in a rush in the mornings, so street vendors and breakfast joints have to get orders out quickly. As a result, many of these recipes are quick and easy to make. From savory to sweet, there are plenty of options to cater to everyone's tastes.

Whenever I go to Taiwan, the flights from Vancouver land early in the morning. The first thing I always do when I get off the plane is head straight to pick up breakfast with my dad. It's become a tradition, and I want to pass along my experiences to you through these yummy recipes.

Taiwanese Savory Egg Crepe

蛋餅

Dan bing

 SERVES 2

Batter

¼ cup all-purpose flour or cake flour

2 tablespoons tapioca starch

½ teaspoon salt

½ teaspoon ground white pepper

½ cup water

1 scallion, both white and green parts, chopped

1 tablespoon olive oil, divided

2 large eggs, beaten

Fillings (optional)

2 thin slices ham (2 ounces / 56g total)

1 cup shredded mozzarella cheese

½ cup fresh or thawed frozen corn kernels

½ cup dried pork fluff or pork floss

For serving

Vegetarian oyster sauce

Chili Oil (page 245) or your favorite brand

An all-time classic Taiwanese breakfast, this savory crepe epitomizes the busy morning rush. So quick and simple to make, but also nutritious and delicious. If you ask a Taiwanese person to think of one breakfast dish, it's highly likely they will say Taiwanese egg crepe. In Mandarin, we call this 蛋餅 dan bing, which literally means "egg crepe." In this recipe, I use scallion pancakes as the wrapping, giving the perfect balance of crispy on the outside and soft on the inside.

When we immigrated to Canada and I was craving a traditional Taiwanese breakfast, my mom would always make this for me. This is also the first breakfast recipe that I learned how to cook on my own, so it holds a special place in my heart. It takes less than 20 minutes to make, and you can customize the filling based on what you have in the fridge—whether it be with corn, cheese, ham, or whatever else your heart desires.

1. **Make the batter:** In a medium bowl, stir together the flour, tapioca starch, salt, white pepper, and water until the batter is a runny consistency with no lumps. Stir in the scallions.

2. **Cook the crepes and assemble:** Heat about 1 teaspoon of the olive oil in a medium nonstick frying pan over medium-high heat. When the pan is hot, pour half the batter into the pan and tilt or swirl the pan to evenly coat the bottom with a thin layer. Cook the crepe for 2 to 3 minutes, until the top is set and the mixture is cooked through. Flip and cook until the crepe starts to brown on the bottom, 1 to 2 minutes. Transfer the crepe to a plate. Repeat with a drizzle of olive oil and the remaining batter.

3. Drizzle a little more olive oil into the pan (no need to wipe the pan). Pour half the beaten eggs into the pan and tilt or swirl the pan to evenly coat the bottom with a thin layer. Place one crepe, browned-side down, on top of the egg, gently press it down with a spatula, and cook until the egg is stuck to the crepe and the bottom starts to brown, 30 to 60 seconds. Flip the crepe, then top with your fillings of choice. Slide the crepe onto a large plate and roll it up into a log. Use a pair of cooking shears to cut into bite-size pieces. Repeat with the remaining crepe and egg. Serve with the vegetarian oyster sauce or chili oil.

Cheesy Baked Pasta

焗肉醬義大利麵

Ju rou jiang yida li mian

SERVES 2

1 tablespoon olive oil

8 ounces / 225g ground beef

2 tablespoons light soy sauce

½ cup chopped yellow onion

1 tablespoon minced garlic

2 tablespoons grated peeled carrot

2 tablespoons tomato paste

2 tablespoons ketchup

1 tablespoon Worcestershire sauce

2 tablespoons sugar

1½ teaspoons ground black pepper

1 teaspoon dried oregano

½ teaspoon dried rosemary

1½ cups chicken stock

1 package (16 ounces / 454g) dried spaghetti

1 cup grated cheddar cheese

My mom created this recipe soon after we immigrated to Canada. She saw how much my sister and I loved American food but she gave this her own spin by adding ketchup and soy sauce to the sauce. This dish captures our childhood in a nutshell—our mom adapting and creating new recipes based on new dishes we were trying in our new home in Canada, but also using familiar ingredients and tastes from Taiwan. Baked pastas are nothing new, even among certain Asian cuisines, but I *promise* you will love my family's rendition with a twist.

1. Preheat the oven to 380°F / 195°C.

2. Heat the olive oil in a large frying pan over medium heat. Add the ground beef and light soy sauce and sauté for 3 to 4 minutes, until the meat is brown. Add the onion, garlic, and carrots and sauté for another 3 minutes, or until the onion is soft and translucent.

3. Add the tomato paste, ketchup, Worcestershire sauce, sugar, black pepper, oregano, and rosemary and stir to combine. Pour in the chicken stock, stir, and simmer over medium heat for 15 minutes, or until the vegetables are tender.

4. Meanwhile, cook the pasta according to the package directions until just al dente. Drain.

5. Transfer the cooked pasta to a large baking dish. Pour the meat sauce over the pasta and stir together. Sprinkle the grated cheese evenly over the top. Bake for 10 minutes, until the cheese is melted and golden brown. Let sit for 5 minutes before serving.

The Ultimate Chicken Chow Mein

雞肉炒麵

Jirou chao mian

SERVES 2

Chow Mein

1½ tablespoons light soy sauce

2 tablespoons cornstarch

½ teaspoon ground white pepper

2 boneless, skinless chicken thighs (6 ounces / 170g total), cut crosswise into thin strips

1 package (8 ounces / 225g) fresh thin chow mein noodles

1 tablespoon olive oil

½ large yellow onion, thinly sliced

1 cup thinly sliced shiitake mushrooms

¼ cup thinly sliced peeled carrot

2 stalks celery, finely chopped

¼ cup finely shredded white cabbage

2 scallions, both white and green parts, cut into 2-inch pieces

Sauce

3 tablespoons light soy sauce

3 tablespoons black vinegar

2½ tablespoons vegetarian oyster sauce

1 tablespoon sesame oil

1 tablespoon sugar

½ teaspoon ground black pepper

There is something about American Chinese food that hits the spot every time! This recipe for one of my favorite comfort foods is not only easy to make but also doesn't break the bank. When I say I had this *at least* two times a week as a university student, I am not kidding. This recipe is also great for meal prepping a day ahead because chow mein tastes great the next day.

This recipe has everything you need for a full meal: you have protein, carbs, and veggies all in one easy dish. Plus, like so many of my recipes, you can easily adjust it based on whatever ingredients or leftovers you have on hand. Easy and satisfying, I guarantee you will be making this chicken chow mein as often as I did.

1. **Marinate the chicken:** In a medium bowl, stir together the light soy sauce, cornstarch, and white pepper until smooth. Add the chicken strips, turning to coat, and let marinate for 10 minutes at room temperature.

2. **Meanwhile, prepare the noodles:** Soak the chow mein noodles for 30 to 60 seconds in a large bowl of hot water. Drain the noodles, rinse under cold running water, then drain again. Set aside. This will keep the noodles nice and chewy and prevent them from being overcooked in the wok.

3. **Make the sauce:** In a small bowl, stir together the light soy sauce, black vinegar, vegetarian oyster sauce, sesame oil, sugar, and black pepper.

4. **Stir-fry and finish the chow mein:** Heat the olive oil in a large wok over medium-high heat. Add the yellow onions and mushrooms and stir-fry for 2 to 3 minutes, until the onions start to soften. Add the chicken and sauté until brown on both sides, another 2 to 3 minutes. Add the carrots and celery and sauté for 1 to 2 minutes, until the celery is translucent. Add the cabbage and sauté for another 2 to 3 minutes, until the cabbage is soft.

5. Increase the heat to high. Add the noodles, drizzle on the sauce, and sauté for 2 to 3 minutes, or until all the sauce is mixed into the noodles. Top with the scallions and sauté for 1 minute. Serve immediately.

飯
Rice

When I was growing up, my grandma would always call me 飯桶 Fan Tong—which literally translates to "rice bucket" but means "rice queen"—because I loved rice so much. To this day, rice is still my go-to for almost every meal. The biggest staple of Asian cuisine, rice is just so versatile, filling, and easy to incorporate into delicious meals. If it were up to me, I'd have rice for breakfast, lunch, and dinner!

Rice is so essential in our family that when we immigrated to Canada, my mom held a rice cooker on her lap for the entire flight over. Funnily enough, when I moved away for university, I carried a rice cooker on my lap for the entire plane ride as well!

Here are some of my essential rice dishes that I'm always making, whether I'm hosting my friends and family or just having a chill night in.

Prawn and Pineapple Fried Rice

鳳梨蝦仁炒飯

Fengli xiaren chaofan

SERVES 2

8 ounces / 225g prawns, peeled and deveined

Marinade

1 teaspoon cornstarch

½ teaspoon curry powder

¼ teaspoon ground white pepper

1½ teaspoons light soy sauce

Pineapple Fried Rice

1½ tablespoons oyster sauce

1½ tablespoons light soy sauce

2½ teaspoons curry powder

1 teaspoon ground white pepper

1 teaspoon sugar

1 tablespoon olive oil

2 garlic cloves, chopped

1 fresh red Thai chili, chopped (optional)

½ shallot, chopped

2 scallions, chopped, white and green parts separated

2 large eggs, beaten

2½ cups cold cooked short-grain rice (page 241)

¼ cup frozen peas

¼ cup frozen corn kernels

½ cup chopped fresh pineapple

I invented this recipe when I was living on my own and trying to use up all the leftovers I had in the fridge. When you're a college student, you're always thinking about what is cheap, is fast to make, and can fill you up, and also how you can make enough in bulk so there's some for the next day. I was constantly making fried rice and I wanted to spice up my meals, so I decided to add some curry powder for spice, pineapple for sweetness, and shrimp for protein.

This is one of those fried rice dishes that is so simple to make, yet when you eat it, it really tastes like a gourmet meal. Whenever I made this for my roommates, they were all *so* impressed—and I hope you are too!

1. **Marinate the shrimp:** In a large bowl, stir together the cornstarch, curry powder, white pepper, and light soy sauce until smooth. Toss the shrimp in the mixture to evenly coat and let marinate for 10 minutes at room temperature.

2. **Make the pineapple fried rice:** In a small bowl, stir together the oyster sauce, light soy sauce, curry powder, white pepper, and sugar. Set aside.

3. Heat the olive oil in a large wok over medium-high heat. Add the shrimp and sauté for 1 minute on each side, or until golden brown. Transfer the shrimp to a plate and set aside.

4. To the wok, add the garlic, chili (if using), shallots, and the scallion whites. Sauté over medium-high heat for 2 to 3 minutes, until fragrant. Add the eggs and sauté for 1 to 2 minutes, until the eggs are fully cooked.

5. Add the rice and the oyster sauce mixture and sauté for 2 to 3 minutes, while breaking apart the rice, until the rice is evenly coated with sauce. Increase the heat to high and add the peas, corn, pineapple, and cooked shrimp. Sauté for 1 to 2 minutes, until the sauce is fully incorporated.

6. Add the scallion greens and sauté for another 30 seconds. Serve immediately.

Buttery Seafood Fried Rice

奶油海鮮炒飯

Naiyou haixian chaofan

SERVES 2

1 skinless salmon fillet (6 ounces / 170g), patted dry

½ teaspoon garlic powder

¼ teaspoon salt

¼ teaspoon ground black pepper

1 tablespoon olive oil

3 tablespoons unsalted butter, divided

4 ounces / 115g sea scallops

4 ounces / 115g thawed frozen baby octopus

4 ounces / 115g prawns, peeled and deveined

1 scallion, chopped, white and green parts separated

2½ cups cooked and cooled short-grain rice (page 241)

1½ teaspoons light soy sauce

½ teaspoon ground white pepper

½ teaspoon dashi powder

2 tablespoons masago (fish roe), for garnish

If you're a beginner in the kitchen and you're looking to treat yourself or spice up date night, you *need* to try my buttery seafood fried rice! It makes perfect use of fancier ingredients—like dashi and masago—and tastes like an expensive seafood fried rice dish you'd get at a restaurant. You can substitute the seafood in this recipe based on your preferences. I like using scallops, prawns, and salmon. Every bite is packed with umami flavor from all the fresh seafood. The secret ingredient that brings this whole dish together is actually butter! This Taiwanese and Japanese fusion recipe is one of my husband Dom's favorites.

1. Season both sides of the salmon with the garlic powder, salt, and black pepper.

2. Heat the olive oil in a large frying pan over medium-high heat. Place the salmon skinned-side down in the pan and fry until cooked through, 4 minutes per side. Transfer the salmon to a plate and use a fork to break it up into small pieces. Wipe the pan.

3. In the same pan, melt 1 tablespoon of the butter over medium heat. Once the butter is melted, add the scallops, octopus, and prawns and fry until the prawns start to turn pink, 2 to 3 minutes. Transfer the seafood to the plate with the salmon and set aside. Wipe the pan.

4. In the same pan, melt the remaining 2 tablespoons butter. Add the scallion whites and sauté for 1 minute. Add the cooked rice, light soy sauce, white pepper, and dashi powder. Break apart the rice, making sure every piece of rice is coated in butter.

5. Add the cooked salmon and seafood. Increase the heat to high, add the scallion greens, and sauté until the rice is golden brown, 2 to 3 minutes. Garnish with the masago. Serve immediately.

Creamy Baked Mushroom Rice

蘑菇燉飯

Mogu dun fan

 SERVES 2

1 cup thinly sliced shiitake mushrooms

½ cup thinly sliced cremini mushrooms

½ cup thinly sliced shimeji mushrooms

1 tablespoon light soy sauce

3 tablespoons unsalted butter

½ yellow onion, finely chopped

2½ tablespoons all-purpose flour

2 cups heavy (35%) cream or 2% milk

2 tablespoons dashi powder or mushroom powder, divided

1 teaspoon ground white pepper

3 cups cooked and cooled short-grain rice (page 241)

2 large eggs, lightly beaten

½ cup grated cheddar cheese

½ cup grated mozzarella cheese

When I say that I eat rice with almost everything, I am *not* kidding. Rice is so versatile. And if you're a rice lover like me, you always have some leftovers in the fridge. This creamy baked rice dish is a perfect way to turn those leftovers into another yummy meal. I made this recipe a lot when I first started cooking because it's really affordable and quick, and levels up some very simple ingredients. Every grain of rice soaks up all the rich, creamy sauce, making it super satisfying to eat. This baked rice is also a great dish to bring to a potluck, and I promise the cheese pull alone will impress your friends and family.

1.   Preheat the oven to 400°F / 200°C.

2.   In a large frying pan over medium-high heat, combine the shiitake, cremini, and shimeji mushrooms and light soy sauce and sauté for 2 to 3 minutes, until the mushrooms have browned and softened. Transfer the mushrooms to a medium bowl.

3.   Melt the butter in the same pan (no need to wipe the pan) over medium-high heat. Add the onions and sauté for 2 to 3 minutes, until soft and translucent. Sprinkle with the flour and stir until smooth with no lumps.

4.   Reduce the heat to medium. Slowly pour the cream into the pan and gently stir until the sauce thickens, 2 to 3 minutes. Add 1 tablespoon of the dashi powder, the white pepper, and the cooked mushrooms and simmer for 2 minutes.

5.   In a large baking dish, combine the cooked rice, eggs, and the remaining 1 tablespoon dashi powder. Stir until the rice is thoroughly coated in the egg. Pour the mushroom sauce over top. Sprinkle the cheddar and mozzarella cheese evenly over the sauce. Bake for 10 minutes, or until the cheese is melted and lightly browned in spots. Let cool for 5 minutes before serving.

Sesame Chicken Rice

麻油雞飯

Ma you ji fan

SERVES 2

1 tablespoon olive oil

8 ounces / 225g chicken wings and/or drumettes

1 teaspoon salt

1 teaspoon ground black pepper

½ cup thinly sliced oyster mushrooms

½ cup thinly sliced shimeji mushrooms

2 tablespoons sesame oil

1 (2-inch) piece fresh ginger, peeled and thinly sliced lengthwise

½ cup rice wine

2 tablespoons light soy sauce

½ teaspoon ground white pepper

2½ cups cold cooked rice (page 241)

For garnish (optional)

1 tablespoon dried goji berries

1 scallion, both white and green parts, chopped

In the streets of Taiwan in wintertime, you can always smell sesame oil chicken, or 麻油雞 ma you ji, wafting from the vendor stalls and restaurants. Sesame oil plus ginger is one of the most comforting combinations to warm you up in winter.

I love making sesame chicken rice because it essentially combines traditional sesame oil chicken with fried rice. It's filling, easy to pack for a quick meal the next day, and so tasty! If you're vegetarian, you can simply skip the chicken and use different types of mushrooms instead. This is a dish that my grandma would make for me when I was a kid, so every time I make it I'm hit with a wave of nostalgia. I remember when my mom and grandma would make this together in the winter, and how the aromas wafting from the house always made me smile.

1.   Heat the olive oil in a large clay pot or nonstick frying pan over medium-high heat. Add the chicken, salt, and black pepper. Cook, stirring frequently, for 4 to 5 minutes, until golden brown all over. Transfer the chicken to a large plate.

2.   In the same pan (no need to wipe the pan), combine the oyster and shimeji mushrooms and cook over medium-high heat, stirring frequently, until softened and turning brown, 2 to 3 minutes.

3.   Add the sesame oil and ginger and cook, stirring frequently, for 1 to 2 minutes, until fragrant. Return the chicken to the pan and stir in the rice wine, light soy sauce, and white pepper. Simmer for 2 minutes.

4.   Add the cooked rice and stir together. Increase the heat to high and cook, stirring frequently, for 2 to 3 minutes, until the rice soaks up all the sauce. Serve garnished with the goji berries and scallions, if desired.

NOTE: A clay pot helps circulate steam around the food, which makes the meat super tender and aromatic. If you do not have a clay pot, use a large nonstick frying pan.

Taiwanese Egg Fried Rice

蛋炒飯

Dan chaofan

 SERVES 4

5 large eggs

2 teaspoons ground white pepper, divided

½ teaspoon salt, plus a pinch for the eggs

5 cups cold cooked rice (page 241)

6 tablespoons olive oil, divided

6 scallions, chopped, white and green parts separated

1½ teaspoons sugar

1½ tablespoons chicken powder or mushroom powder

1 tablespoon light soy sauce

This is my version of the acclaimed restaurant chain Din Tai Fung's famous egg fried rice. In Taiwan, we have a term for the perfect fried rice: 粒粒分明 li li fen ming. This means you can see every individual grain of rice coated in oil and flavor and it isn't soggy. Fried rice may be easy to make, but two tips can make all the difference between a simple fried rice and an amazing one. First, use cold cooked rice, preferably day-old. If you use hot rice, it will become soggy and stick together. Second, use a generous amount of oil.

This is a straightforward—but delicious!—fried rice, and it pairs well with any recipe in the book. You can use it as your base recipe and add any proteins you like. I recommend ham, shrimp, chicken, or even beef. This recipe is inspired by many restaurants' winning ratio of 1:1:½, an equal amount of salt and sugar, then half the amount of MSG, which gives the dish the perfect balance of flavors. Most people are surprised to learn that sugar is an ingredient in fried rice, but it balances out the saltiness and gives the dish the perfect umami flavor.

1. In a medium bowl, whisk together the eggs, 1 teaspoon of the white pepper, and a pinch of salt. Set aside.

2. Wet your hands and break apart the rice. This will prevent the fried rice from becoming overcooked and soggy.

3. Heat 3 tablespoons of the olive oil in a large wok over medium-high heat. When the wok is hot, add the scallion whites and sauté for 1 minute, until fragrant. Add the eggs and let set for 30 seconds before scrambling the eggs.

4. Add the remaining 3 tablespoons olive oil to the wok. Add the cooked rice and sauté for 2 minutes, separating the rice and ensuring it is evenly coated in the oil.

5. Add the sugar, chicken powder, light soy sauce, the remaining 1 teaspoon white pepper, and the remaining ½ teaspoon salt. Sauté for another 2 minutes.

6. Increase the heat to high. Add the scallion greens and sauté for another 1 minute. Serve immediately.

湯沙拉
Soups and Salads

There is something about Asian soups and salads that is so appetizing. In Mandarin, we have the term 開味 kai wei, which literally means "open stomach" or "open appetite," and there's a reason why appetizers are called 開胃菜 kai wei cai, or "open stomach dish." These soups and salads are the definition of kai wei, as they will open up your appetite and make you want to eat more and more!

Soups and salads are my go-to for lunch because they are so easy, quick, and usually pretty light. You can enjoy these on their own as a meal, or you can prepare some of these salads and soups in bulk and enjoy them as appetizers or side dishes with your main meals throughout the week.

Egg Drop Soup

蛋花湯

Dan hua tang

 SERVES 4

3 large eggs

1 teaspoon ground white pepper, more as needed

A pinch of salt, more as needed

1½ teaspoons olive oil

2 scallions, chopped, white and green parts separated

5 cups vegetable stock or chicken stock

2 tablespoons cornstarch

¼ cup cold water

This is a classic soup in Chinese and Taiwanese culture. It is so simple, yet there are so many tips to make it perfect that I want to share. This is one of the first recipes I taught my husband Dom how to make on his own. The first time we made it together, he was like, "Wow, that's it?" Now he claims that his egg drop soup is even better than most restaurants'! (That just goes to show how easy and foolproof this recipe is, because my husband usually isn't allowed in the kitchen.) Whenever I'm out of town, he'll make himself egg drop soup and heat up some frozen dumplings for a quick and easy meal.

This soup is really comforting—each sip feels like a warm embrace. Every family has their own recipe, but I truly believe my family has perfected this recipe over many generations, and I'm here to pass it along to you. This soup takes less than 10 minutes to prepare, and you likely have all the ingredients at home.

1. In a large bowl, whisk together the eggs, white pepper, and salt. Set aside.

2. Heat the olive oil in a large pot over medium heat. Add the scallion whites, increase the heat to medium-high, and sauté for 2 to 3 minutes, until fragrant.

3. Reduce the heat to medium. Pour in the vegetable stock and simmer for 12 minutes.

4. Meanwhile, in a small measuring cup, stir together the cornstarch and water until smooth.

5. Pour the cornstarch mixture into the pot. Stir well to ensure the cornstarch does not settle at the bottom of the pot. Simmer for 1 minute, or until the soup is thicker. Remove from the heat.

6. Using a ladle, stir the soup in one direction. While stirring, slowly drizzle in the egg mixture from 8 inches above the pot. This prevents the eggs from curdling and separating. Let sit for 30 seconds—do not stir. After 30 seconds use the ladle to gently stir the eggs into the soup.

7. Add more salt or white pepper, if needed. Garnish with the scallion greens and serve immediately.

Hot and Sour Soup

酸辣湯

Suan latang

 SERVES 4

¼ cup black vinegar, more as needed

3 tablespoons light soy sauce

2 teaspoons ground white pepper, more as needed

1 teaspoon sugar

2 cups thinly sliced shiitake mushrooms

½ cup thinly sliced peeled carrot

½ cup canned bamboo shoots, drained, rinsed, and thinly sliced

5 cups vegetable stock or chicken stock

1 package (14 ounces / 396g) soft or medium-firm tofu, cut crosswise into thin strips

2 tablespoons cornstarch

¼ cup cold water

2 eggs, beaten

Chopped fresh cilantro leaves and tender stems, for garnish

I love spicy food and sour food! My mom and I are always joking that we love hot and sour food so much that whenever we order hot and sour soup at restaurants, we always add extra white pepper to spice it up and a lot of black vinegar for an extra-sour taste! Hot and sour soup is super filling. There are so many proteins and vegetables in it that you can easily enjoy this as a full meal.

1. In a small bowl, stir together the black vinegar, light soy sauce, white pepper, and sugar. Add more white pepper (spice) and/or black vinegar (sour), if desired.

2. In a large pot, combine the mushrooms, carrots, bamboo shoots, and vegetable stock. Bring to a simmer over medium heat and cook for 3 to 4 minutes, until the carrots start to soften. Gently add the tofu and cook for another 2 to 3 minutes, until the tofu is slightly browned. Pour in the sauce and simmer for 1 to 2 minutes, until fragrant.

3. Meanwhile, in a small measuring cup, stir together the cornstarch and water until smooth.

4. Pour the cornstarch mixture into the pot. Stir well to ensure the cornstarch does not settle at the bottom of the pot. Simmer for 1 minute, or until the soup is thicker. Remove from the heat.

5. Using a ladle, stir the soup in one direction. While stirring, slowly drizzle in the beaten eggs from 8 inches above the pot. This prevents the eggs from curdling and separating. Let sit for 30 seconds—do not stir. After 30 seconds use the ladle to gently stir the eggs into the soup.

6. Garnish with the cilantro and serve immediately.

NOTE: When I was living on my own, I would cook noodles the next day and have hot and sour soup with noodles for lunch, which is so delicious and filling. Definitely worth trying!

Sesame Chopped Salad

芝麻沙拉

Zhima shala

SERVES 2

Dressing

2½ tablespoons sesame oil

2 tablespoons Chinese sesame paste

1½ tablespoons light soy sauce

1½ tablespoons sugar

1 tablespoon toasted sesame seeds

1½ teaspoons grated peeled fresh ginger

¼ cup olive oil

¼ cup rice vinegar

A pinch each of salt and ground black pepper

Salad

5 cups shredded white cabbage

2 cups shredded red cabbage

1 carrot, peeled and julienned

2 scallions, both white and green parts, chopped

1 cup shredded cooked chicken (optional)

For garnish

Fried wonton strips

Fresh cilantro leaves

I'm not the biggest fan of cold foods, but there's something so refreshing about this sesame chopped salad that I make it all the time during the summer. One of the main reasons is because if I prepare the dressing in bulk, I can have salad on the table in just 5 minutes throughout the week. This dressing works really well with any vegetables, such as lettuce or kale, and you can add any kind of protein you like, such as shredded salmon or turkey. I top it with some super-crunchy wonton chips for extra texture.

1. **Make the dressing:** In a large measuring cup or small bowl, stir together the sesame oil, sesame paste, light soy sauce, sugar, sesame seeds, ginger, olive oil, rice vinegar, salt, and black pepper.

2. **Make and assemble the salad:** In a large bowl, combine the white cabbage, red cabbage, carrots, scallions, and chicken, if using. Pour the dressing over the salad and toss to combine. Garnish with the fried wonton strips and cilantro.

Spicy Chicken Salad

麻辣雞肉沙拉

Mala jirou shala

SERVES 2

Shredded Chicken

1 (2-inch) piece fresh ginger, peeled and cut lengthwise into ¼-inch-thick slices

1 scallion, both white and green parts, chopped

1 teaspoon Sichuan peppercorns

8 ounces / 225g boneless, skinless chicken breast

Sauce

2 tablespoons black vinegar

1½ tablespoons light soy sauce

1½ tablespoons Chili Oil (page 245) or your favorite brand

1½ tablespoons sesame oil

1 teaspoon sugar

1 teaspoon toasted sesame seeds

Salad

1 head romaine lettuce, coarsely chopped

1 large English cucumber, thinly sliced crosswise

1 scallion, both white and green parts, chopped

For garnish

Fresh cilantro leaves

Fried Shallots (page 249)

This salad is the definition of 開胃菜 kai wei cai, which translates as "open stomach dish" or appetizers, that I talked about in the introduction to this section. With crunchy lettuce and cucumber paired with shredded chicken and a spicy sesame sauce, you won't even notice you're eating a salad. This delicious and refreshing dish is popular at bars—known as 啤酒屋 pi jiu wu, or "beer houses"—in Taiwan during the summer because it pairs perfectly with an ice-cold beer.

1. **Prepare the shredded chicken:** In a large pot, combine the ginger, scallions, Sichuan peppercorns, and chicken. Add enough water to cover the chicken and bring to a boil over medium-high heat. Once the water starts boiling, cook for 4 minutes. Remove from the heat, cover with a lid, and let sit for 18 minutes, until the chicken is white and fully cooked. Transfer the chicken to a medium bowl to cool completely. Discard the cooking liquid.

2. Once the chicken has fully cooled, shred it with a fork.

3. **Make the sauce:** In a small bowl, stir together the black vinegar, light soy sauce, chili oil, sesame oil, sugar, and sesame seeds.

4. **Assemble the salad:** In a large bowl, toss together the lettuce, cucumber, scallions, and shredded chicken. Pour the sauce over the salad and toss to combine. Garnish with the cilantro and fried shallots.

NOTE: If you're making this in advance, store the lettuce and cucumbers in a separate container without the sauce to ensure they stay nice and crunchy.

Spicy Lotus Root Salad

麻辣蓮藕沙拉

Mala lianou shala

 SERVES 2

2 ounces / 55g dried wood ear mushrooms

5 ounces / 140g lotus root, peeled and cut crosswise into ⅛-inch-thick slices

5 garlic cloves, minced

6 dried Chinese red chilies

1½ teaspoons red chili flakes

1½ teaspoons sesame seeds

1½ tablespoons Chili Oil (page 245) or your favorite brand

¼ cup vegetable oil

½ teaspoon Sichuan peppercorns

2½ tablespoons black vinegar

2 tablespoons light soy sauce

1½ teaspoons sugar

3 tablespoons chopped fresh cilantro leaves

Unsalted roasted peanuts, for garnish (optional)

Some restaurants in Taiwan will set out appetizers at the front entrance, and I always reach for the lotus root salad. If you ask my friends and family what my favorite vegetable is, *everyone* will say lotus root! Lotus root is actually the stem of the lotus flower. It may look intimidating but it's easy to cook and super versatile. It's crunchy, absorbs flavor well, and reminds me of a less starchy version of potatoes. The best part about this salad is that if you prep it ahead, the lotus root will continue to soak up the flavor of the sauce, so you can enjoy it throughout the week, and it tastes better every time. Lotus root also has plenty of health benefits, such as boosting digestion, regulating blood pressure, and reducing stress.

1. Soak the mushrooms in a bowl of room-temperature water until softened, 15 to 20 minutes. Drain, squeeze dry, and break into bite-size pieces. Set aside.

2. Meanwhile, bring a large pot of water to a rapid boil over high heat. Add the lotus root and blanch for 3 minutes. Drain and set aside. This will help the lotus root stay flavorful and crunchy.

3. In a large heatproof bowl, combine the garlic, Chinese red chilies, red chili flakes, sesame seeds, and chili oil.

4. In a small saucepan, heat the vegetable oil and Sichuan peppercorns over high heat for 1 to 2 minutes, or until the oil reaches 350°F / 180°C on a deep-frying thermometer. Carefully pour the hot oil over the chili mixture. (You can strain the oil into the bowl through a metal strainer to remove the peppercorns, if desired.) Once the oil stops bubbling, stir to combine.

5. Pour the black vinegar, light soy sauce, and sugar into the hot oil. Stir until the sugar is dissolved.

6. Add the lotus root, mushrooms, and cilantro to the sauce and toss. Transfer the salad to a large serving bowl. Garnish with the roasted peanuts, if desired, and serve immediately.

主菜
Entrées

The recipes in this section will teach you ways to cook various proteins for your meals, and you can pair them with whatever you'd like, whether it be plain rice, noodles, or salad. These are my favorite essential staple recipes that are always on rotation in my weekday meal repertoire. They include a combination of traditional recipes that you'd find at Taiwanese night markets, along with a lot of fun fusion recipes that I have developed over the years.

Have fun mixing and matching these recipes with whatever suits your tastes. Even though they are all super easy for weeknight dinners, they're also great for treating yourself, for date night, or for hosting friends and family.

Miso Honey-Glazed Salmon

味噌蜜汁鮭魚

Weizeng mi zhi guiyu

SERVES 2

2 skin-on salmon fillets (7 ounces / 200g each), patted dry

1 teaspoon salt

1 teaspoon ground black pepper

2½ tablespoons all-purpose flour

3½ tablespoons light soy sauce

3 tablespoons mirin or liquid honey

2½ tablespoons sake

1 tablespoon white miso

1 tablespoon sugar

1½ teaspoons olive oil

For garnish

Toasted sesame seeds

Chopped scallions, both white and green parts

I love pairing salmon with miso because it is healthy and super delicious. And I'm all for healthy and delicious foods! Miso has so many health benefits. Not only is it rich in nutrients and vitamins, it's also high in probiotics, which means it helps the body maintain healthy bacteria levels, which in turn promotes gut health and enhances your immune system. This dish can be enjoyed over rice or with a salad. Miso is fermented, so its flavor is quite salty, and this recipe includes mirin or honey to balance that out. (I like to marinate my salmon in bulk and freeze it so that it's ready to go throughout the week.)

1. Season the flesh side of the salmon with the salt and black pepper. Dust both sides of the salmon with the flour, shaking off any excess.

2. In a small bowl, stir together the light soy sauce, mirin, sake, miso, and sugar.

3. Heat the olive oil in a large frying pan over medium-high heat. Place the salmon skin-side down in the pan and cook for 1½ to 2 minutes, until the skin starts to brown. Flip and cook for another 1½ to 2 minutes. The salmon should not be fully cooked. Transfer the salmon to a plate.

4. In the same pan (no need to wipe the pan) over medium-low heat, drizzle in the sauce and simmer for 1 minute.

5. Add the salmon skin-side down and cook for another 2 to 3 minutes, until it starts to absorb the sauce. Transfer the salmon to a large plate and spoon the sauce over top. Garnish with the sesame seeds and scallions. Serve immediately.

Sweet and Sour Tofu

糖醋豆腐

Tang cu doufu

 SERVES 2

1 package (1 pound / 450g) medium-firm tofu, cut into bite-size cubes

2 tablespoons salt

1½ cups tapioca starch

½ teaspoon ground white pepper

1 cup canola oil

1½ tablespoons minced garlic

3 tablespoons ketchup

2½ tablespoons rice vinegar

2 tablespoons light soy sauce

2 tablespoons vegetarian oyster sauce

1 tablespoon plum sauce

1½ teaspoons sugar

For garnish

Toasted sesame seeds

Chopped scallions, green part only

One thing I *always* have in my fridge is tofu. Tofu is such a great protein because it's healthy and really soaks up flavors. It also cooks fast and is super versatile. I created this recipe for a friend of mine in university who had never had sweet and sour chicken because she was vegetarian. I will never forget my friend's reaction when she took her first bite—she was blown away by all the flavors and even packed up all the leftovers to go! This recipe is both vegetarian and gluten-free. Pair it with my fried rice or chow mein and you have yourself some takeout at home!

1. In a medium bowl, soak the tofu in the salt and 2 cups of water for 10 minutes. Make sure all the tofu is covered in water. The brine will draw out excess moisture from the tofu, helping it become crispy and flavorful when cooked. Drain the tofu and pat dry with a paper towel.

2. In a large bowl, stir together the tapioca starch and white pepper. Add the tofu and gently toss to coat completely. Let the tofu sit in the mixture for 5 minutes to ensure the coating sticks.

3. Heat the canola oil in a large frying pan over medium-high heat. Add the tofu and fry for 7 to 8 minutes, stirring every 30 seconds, until crispy and golden brown all over. Using a spider or slotted spoon, transfer the tofu to a large plate. Pour out the oil and wipe the pan.

4. In a small bowl, stir together the garlic, ketchup, rice vinegar, light soy sauce, vegetarian oyster sauce, plum sauce, and sugar.

5. Add the sauce into the same pan and simmer over medium heat for 1 to 2 minutes, until it thickens. Add the crispy fried tofu, increase the heat to high, and sauté for 1 minute, turning to coat with the sauce.

6. Transfer to a plate and garnish with the sesame seeds and scallions. Serve immediately.

Spicy Honey Orange Shrimp

香辣蜂蜜蝦

Xiang la fengmi xia

SERVES 4

1½ cups tapioca starch

1 tablespoon garlic powder

1 teaspoon salt

1 teaspoon ground black pepper

7 ounces / 200g shrimp or prawns, peeled and deveined

1 tablespoon orange zest

½ cup orange juice

3½ tablespoons liquid honey

2½ tablespoons light soy sauce

1½ tablespoons oyster sauce

1½ tablespoons minced garlic

1½ teaspoons grated peeled fresh ginger

1 teaspoon red chili flakes

½ cup canola oil, for frying

2 tablespoons cornstarch

3 tablespoons cold water

Chopped scallions, both white and green parts, for garnish

If you're looking for a really satisfying weeknight dinner, this is it. This dish has the perfect balance of flavors, and you'll be licking your fingers throughout the meal! This is another recipe I came up with when I was learning to cook. Whenever shrimp was on sale, I always bought lots and stashed it in the freezer—something I still do today!

Shrimp cooks very fast and is so easy to prepare. I love pairing this dish with a bed of fluffy white rice, but it also works well with noodles or chow mein.

1. In a large bowl, stir together the tapioca starch, garlic powder, salt, and black pepper. Add the shrimp and toss to evenly coat. Let the shrimp sit in the mixture for 5 minutes to ensure the coating sticks.

2. In a medium bowl, stir together the orange zest, orange juice, honey, light soy sauce, oyster sauce, garlic, ginger, and red chili flakes.

3. Heat the canola oil in a large frying pan over medium-high heat until it reaches 350°F / 180°C on a deep-frying thermometer. Add the shrimp to the hot oil and fry for 2 to 3 minutes per side, until golden brown. Using a spider or metal tongs, transfer the shrimp to a plate lined with paper towel to absorb excess oil. Pour out the oil and wipe the pan.

4. Reduce the heat to medium. Pour the sauce into the same pan and simmer for 2 to 3 minutes, until fragrant.

5. In a small measuring cup, stir together the cornstarch and water until smooth.

6. Pour the cornstarch mixture into the sauce and stir until combined. Simmer the sauce for 1 minute, or until it has thickened. Increase the heat to high, add the shrimp to the sauce, and sauté for another 1 minute.

7. Transfer to a plate and garnish with the scallions. Serve immediately.

Mushroom and Chicken Sizzling Plate

蘑菇鐵板雞

Mogu tie ban ji

SERVES 2

3 tablespoons unsalted butter, divided

½ yellow onion, roughly chopped

1 shallot, roughly chopped

2 cups thinly sliced cremini mushrooms

1½ tablespoons minced garlic

2½ tablespoons Worcestershire sauce

2½ tablespoons vegetarian oyster sauce

2 tablespoons ketchup

1 tablespoon light soy sauce

2 teaspoons ground black pepper, divided

1 teaspoon sugar

1½ tablespoons cornstarch

3 tablespoons cold water

1 cup chicken stock

2 boneless, skin-on chicken thighs (3 ounces / 85g each), patted dry

1 teaspoon salt

2 tablespoons olive oil, divided

9 ounces / 250g cooked spaghetti

2 fried eggs (optional)

This Taiwanese night market classic is the dream meal that everyone needs to try! It's also known as 鐵板雞 tie ban ji, or "iron plate chicken": a savory, creamy mushroom sauce is drizzled on top of tender pan-fried chicken and topped with a fried egg—all on a sizzling cast-iron plate. At the markets you can smell the sizzling plates at the stalls from blocks away. When I first moved to Canada, I had such a hard time re-creating this recipe. I tested so many different versions, but this one really brings me back home. Don't worry if you don't have a sizzling plate at home. Just make this in a pan on the stovetop and transfer everything to a regular plate.

1. Melt 2 tablespoons of the butter in a large pot over medium heat. Add the onions and shallots and sauté for 1 to 2 minutes, until fragrant.

2. Add the mushrooms and garlic and sauté for 2 to 3 minutes, until the mushrooms are soft.

3. Add the Worcestershire sauce, vegetarian oyster sauce, ketchup, light soy sauce, 1 teaspoon of the black pepper, sugar, and the remaining 1 tablespoon butter. Stir to combine.

4. In a small measuring cup, stir together the cornstarch and water until smooth.

5. Add the chicken stock to the mushrooms and simmer for 2 to 3 minutes, until fragrant. Give the cornstarch mixture a stir, pour it into the pot, and stir well. Simmer for 2 to 3 minutes, until the sauce has thickened.

6. Season the chicken with the salt and the remaining 1 teaspoon black pepper. Heat 1 tablespoon of the olive oil in a medium frying pan over medium-high heat. Place the chicken in the pan and cook for 2 minutes on each side, or until the meat is no longer pink.

7. Meanwhile, heat the remaining 1 tablespoon olive oil in a large cast-iron sizzling plate (see Note) over high heat. Place the cooked noodles into the pan and transfer the chicken skin side up on top of the noodles.

8. Once the chicken starts to brown, drizzle the garlic mushroom sauce over top and let it sizzle until the chicken is cooked through. If desired, slice the chicken before serving. Top with the fried eggs, if using.

NOTE: If you do not have a sizzling plate, finish cooking the chicken in the frying pan, adding the noodles, egg, and sauce to the pan. Transfer to a plate.

Taiwanese XXL Fried Chicken

台灣特大號雞排

Taiwan teda hao jipai

SERVES 2

Seasoning Powder

½ teaspoon chili powder

½ teaspoon five-spice powder

½ teaspoon garlic powder

¼ teaspoon hot paprika

¼ teaspoon ground white pepper

A pinch of salt

Fried Chicken

¼ cup rice wine or beer

3 tablespoons light soy sauce

1 tablespoon vegetarian oyster sauce

1½ tablespoons five-spice powder

1 teaspoon ground white pepper

1½ tablespoons minced garlic

2 boneless, skinless chicken breasts (4 ounces / 115g each), butterflied and flattened with the back of a knife or meat tenderizer

¼ cup rice flour

1 large egg, beaten

2½ cups tapioca starch, for dredging

3 cups canola oil, for frying

One of the most famous Taiwanese street foods is juicy Taiwanese XXL fried chicken. XXL is a term for oversized dishes that are very popular in Taiwan. Some of my best childhood memories are of walking through the night market with XXL fried chicken in one hand, a cold drink in the other. You will see a ton of stalls selling XXL fried chicken in every Taiwanese night market, with lengthy lineups at each one because it's so popular! This dish is gluten-free, since it uses tapioca starch instead of flour. This is also the reason why it's not too heavy like other fried chicken recipes, even though it's so big and packed with batter. The star is the seasoning powder dusted on top, made from different spices such as five-spice powder, red chili powder, and white pepper.

1. **Make the seasoning powder:** In a small bowl, stir together the chili powder, five-spice powder, garlic powder, paprika, white pepper, and salt. Set aside.

2. **Marinate the chicken:** In a large bowl, stir together the rice wine, light soy sauce, vegetarian oyster sauce, five-spice powder, white pepper, and garlic. Submerge the chicken in the marinade. Let sit for 20 minutes at room temperature.

3. Add the rice flour and egg and mix well. Make sure the chicken is fully coated with the batter.

4. Evenly sprinkle the tapioca starch onto a large plate. Take each piece of chicken from the marinade and dredge through the tapioca starch, completely coating both sides. Let sit for 5 to 7 minutes on the same plate to prevent the coating from falling off during frying.

5. When you are ready to fry the chicken, heat the canola oil in a large pot or deep-fryer over medium-high heat until it reaches 350°F / 180°C on a deep-frying thermometer. Using metal tongs, transfer the chicken breasts, one at a time, to the hot oil. Fry for 8 to 10 minutes, until golden brown and crispy on both sides. Transfer the chicken to a plate. Heat the oil over high heat until it reaches 380°F / 195°C, then use tongs to return the chicken to the pot. Fry for another 1 minute.

6. Transfer the fried chicken to a large plate and season both sides with the seasoning powder. Serve immediately.

Buttery Napa Cabbage

奶油白菜

Naiyou baicai

 SERVES 4

2 tablespoons unsalted butter

2 tablespoons all-purpose flour

1 cup heavy (35%) cream

1½ teaspoons minced garlic

1½ teaspoons dashi powder or mushroom powder

1 teaspoon ground white pepper

A pinch of salt

1 large napa cabbage (2 pounds / 900g), cut into 1-inch pieces

1 cup shredded mozzarella cheese

If you know someone who doesn't like cabbage, you *have* to make this dish for them. It's so creamy, rich, and melt-in-the-mouth, I promise they will instantly fall in love with cabbage. This is one of my signature dishes and I always bring it to dinner parties. Also known as creamy cabbage, it is a very common recipe in Taiwan as it is many moms' favorite way to get their kids to eat their veggies. Napa cabbage is great at absorbing flavors from sauces; in this case, it soaks up all the creamy umami sauce, then gets topped with cheese and baked. A perfect fusion of Western-style casserole and Asian flavors.

1. Preheat the oven to 400°F / 200°C.

2. Melt the butter in a large frying pan over medium heat. Add the flour and cook the roux, stirring, for 2 to 3 minutes. The roux should be thick and smooth, with no raw flour smell left.

3. Slowly add the cream while stirring constantly, until the sauce begins to boil and thicken. Add the garlic, dashi powder, white pepper, and salt. Reduce the heat to low and simmer, stirring constantly, for another 2 minutes.

4. Add the cabbage and mix well. Cover with a lid and cook for 3 to 4 minutes, until the cabbage softens. Transfer the mixture to a large baking dish and sprinkle with the cheese.

5. Bake for 10 minutes, or until the cheese has fully melted. Let sit for 2 or 3 minutes before serving.

Eggplant with Pork

茄子豬肉

Qiezi zhurou

SERVES 2 TO 3

2 Chinese eggplants

2 tablespoons white vinegar

1 cup olive oil, divided, for frying

3 ounces / 85g ground pork or chicken

2 tablespoons minced garlic

1 scallion, chopped, white and green parts separated

1 dried red Thai chili, chopped

2½ tablespoons vegetarian oyster sauce

1 tablespoon light soy sauce

1½ teaspoons sugar

I will be the first to admit that for a long time I was not a big fan of eggplant. My mom used to have to force me to eat it because I simply refused. I don't know whether it was the color, the shape, or the texture, but I just didn't like it. However, being the huge foodie I am, I was tempted to try it when I went to a stir-fry restaurant in Taiwan where this eggplant looked and smelled so good. One bite and I instantly fell in love and knew I needed to create my own recipe. I even asked the chef what the secret was to keeping the eggplant so purple, and he told me it was soaking it in vinegar.

1. Trim the ends off the eggplants and cut lengthwise into quarters. Cut the quarters into 2-inch-long pieces.

2. In a large bowl, soak the eggplant in the vinegar and 3 cups of water for 10 minutes, making sure the eggplant is fully submerged. This will prevent the eggplant from turning brown. Drain and rinse with cold water.

3. Heat ¾ cup of the olive oil in a medium frying pan over medium-high heat. Add the eggplant and fry for 2 minutes per side, until it starts to brown. Transfer the eggplant to a plate.

4. Heat the remaining ¼ cup olive oil in a large frying pan over medium-high heat. Add the pork and sauté for 3 to 4 minutes, breaking the meat apart, until the meat is no longer pink. Add the garlic, scallion whites, and chili. Sauté for another 1 to 2 minutes, until the meat starts to brown.

5. Increase the heat to high and add the eggplant, vegetarian oyster sauce, light soy sauce, and sugar. Sauté for another 2 to 3 minutes, until the eggplant absorbs the sauce. Transfer to a large plate and garnish with the scallion greens. Serve immediately.

Braised Soy Sauce Chicken

滷雞腿

Lu jitui

SERVES 2

2 bone-in, skin-on chicken legs
(8 ounces / 225g total)

½ cup light soy sauce

¼ cup dark soy sauce

3 tablespoons rice wine

3 tablespoons sugar

2 star anise pods

1 bay leaf

5 garlic cloves, peeled and smashed

1 whole scallion

2 cups water, more as needed

Taiwanese bento boxes often include braised soy sauce chicken. I make this a lot because it's super easy and really affordable. The chicken is so tender that it falls off the bone, and the sauce is delectable. In fact, I love to drizzle the sauce over rice or vegetables every time I make this dish.

For a recipe like this, I highly recommend using the dark meat of the chicken, such as whole legs, drumsticks, or thighs, because braising tends to dry out the light breast meat. It's also preferable to use chicken with the skin on, as the skin not only adds flavor to the broth but also helps keep the meat juicy and tender.

1. In a medium pot, combine the chicken, light soy sauce, dark soy sauce, rice wine, sugar, star anise, bay leaf, garlic, scallion, and water. The chicken should be fully submerged in the liquid; if not, add more water.

2. Bring to a simmer over medium-high heat and cook for 5 minutes. Cover with a lid, reduce the heat to low, and simmer for 15 minutes, turning the chicken halfway through, until both sides are browned and the internal temperature reaches 170°F / 77°C.

3. Transfer the chicken to a large serving plate. Drizzle the sauce over the chicken and serve immediately.

Taiwanese Braised Pork Chops

台式滷排骨

Taishi lu pai gu

SERVES 2

2 bone-in pork chops (4 ounces / 115g each)

1 tablespoon five-spice powder

1 teaspoon ground white pepper

A pinch each of salt and ground black pepper

¼ cup cornstarch

1 large egg, beaten

1 cup tapioca starch

½ cup canola oil, for frying

¼ cup light soy sauce

1½ tablespoons vegetarian oyster sauce

1 tablespoon sugar

4 garlic cloves, peeled and smashed

1 bay leaf

2 star anise pods

1 cup water

I used to get so excited when we visited my grandma because we would take the train, which meant I could order a bento box. Train bentos in Taiwan are so popular, as they are affordable and delicious, have great portions, and are packed with meat, vegetables, and rice. If you ever visit, they are definitely a must-try! There are so many different flavors and styles of bento boxes, but my top choice has always been 滷排骨 lu pai gu, or Taiwanese braised pork chops.

The trick with the pork chops is to first pan-fry them until crispy on both sides, then simmer until the batter soaks in all the juices while keeping the pork from being overcooked and dry. This pork is so addictive that you're going to want bowls and bowls of rice! Enjoy with my Garlic Cucumber Salad (page 97).

1. Prepare the pork chops by making cuts along the fat, about 1 inch apart. This will prevent the pork from curling up while frying. Using the back of a knife or a meat tenderizer, flatten the pork to about ½ inch thick.

2. In a large bowl, combine the pork chops, five-spice powder, white pepper, salt and black pepper, cornstarch, and egg. Using your hands, massage the mixture all over the pork until well coated. Leave the pork in the bowl and let marinate for 10 minutes at room temperature.

3. Evenly sprinkle the tapioca starch onto a plate. Take each pork chop from the marinade and dredge through the tapioca starch, completely coating both sides. Let sit for 10 minutes on the same plate to prevent the coating from falling off during frying.

4. Heat the canola oil in a large frying pan over medium-high heat. Add the pork chops one at a time and fry for 2 to 3 minutes per side, until lightly golden brown. Transfer to a plate lined with paper towel to absorb excess oil. Pour out the oil and wipe the pan.

5. In the same pan over medium heat, combine the light soy sauce, vegetarian oyster sauce, sugar, garlic, bay leaf, star anise, and water. Simmer for 2 to 3 minutes, until fragrant. Add the pork chops to the sauce and simmer for 15 minutes.

6. Transfer to a plate and serve immediately.

Black Pepper Beef Short Ribs

黑胡椒牛小排

Hei hejiao niu xiao pai

SERVES 4

1½ pounds / 675g flanken-style ribs (about 3 strips), patted dry

1 teaspoon salt

2½ teaspoons ground black pepper, divided, more as needed

1½ teaspoons olive oil

1½ tablespoons minced garlic

3 tablespoons vegetarian oyster sauce

2½ tablespoons ketchup

2 tablespoons light soy sauce

2 tablespoons liquid honey

1½ tablespoons unsalted butter

Chopped scallions, both white and green parts, for garnish

Steakhouses in Taiwan are well known for their black pepper sauce, which has a kick of spiciness that blends perfectly with the sweetness of honey and ketchup. The best combination with beef, in my opinion, is black pepper, butter, and soy sauce. When I moved to Canada, it took me a while to figure out what the missing ingredient was, until I realized it was the tartness from ketchup. Ketchup gives the sauce a nice tang and also provides a little bit of sweetness that pairs surprisingly well with the beef. My husband Dom absolutely loves beef; he remembers having this dish all the time growing up.

1. Season the ribs on both sides with the salt and 1 teaspoon of the black pepper.

2. Heat the olive oil in a large frying pan over medium-high heat. Add the beef and fry for 2 to 3 minutes per side, until browned. Transfer the beef to a large plate. Wipe the pan.

3. In a small bowl, stir together the garlic, vegetarian oyster sauce, ketchup, light soy sauce, honey, and the remaining 1½ teaspoons black pepper.

4. In the same frying pan, melt the butter over medium heat. Pour the sauce into the pan and simmer for 1 minute.

5. Add the beef to the sauce, increase the heat to medium-high, and cook for 1 to 2 minutes per side, until the sauce is absorbed into the meat.

6. Transfer to a plate and garnish with the scallions. Serve immediately.

NOTE: Flanken-style ribs are a style of short ribs that are cut across the bones. You can find them at most butchers.

Mushrooms and Bok Choy

蒜蓉蘑菇白菜

Suan rong mogu baicai

 SERVES 4

¼ cup light soy sauce

2 tablespoons vegetarian oyster sauce

1 tablespoon sugar

2 garlic cloves, peeled and smashed

2 cups water

8 ounces / 225g shiitake mushrooms (about 10 large mushrooms)

2 teaspoons salt

1 teaspoon vegetable oil

8 baby bok choy, cut lengthwise into ½-inch-thick pieces

2 tablespoons cornstarch

¼ cup water

1 tablespoon sesame oil

Dried goji berries, for garnish (optional)

Bok choy is an extremely popular vegetable in Asian cuisine. Not only is it easy to cook, it's packed with plenty of nutrients. It's a good source of vitamin C, is rich in antioxidants, and can support heart, bone, and thyroid health. It's also good for your skin (now who doesn't love that?). Every Lunar New Year, you will see this mushroom and bok choy dish on the table. It's one recipe that I always make at the New Year because it's so simple, quick to make, and both healthy and delicious. It's also a great way to get your vegetables in!

1.   In a large pot, combine the light soy sauce, vegetarian oyster sauce, sugar, garlic, and water and bring to a simmer over medium-low heat. Add the mushrooms and simmer, uncovered, for 15 minutes, until the mushrooms start to soften.

2.   Meanwhile, bring a separate large pot of water to a rapid boil over medium-high heat. Add the salt, vegetable oil, and bok choy and blanch for 2 to 3 minutes, until the bok choy is soft. Using a spider or metal tongs, transfer the bok choy to a large plate. Discard the cooking liquid.

3.   Once the mushrooms are soft, use a slotted spoon to remove them from the cooking liquid and place them on top of the bok choy.

4.   In a small measuring cup, stir together the cornstarch and water until smooth.

5.   Pour the cornstarch mixture into the mushroom sauce and stir well to ensure the cornstarch does not settle at the bottom of the pot. Simmer for another 1 minute, or until the sauce has thickened. Add the sesame oil and stir until combined.

6.   Drizzle the sauce over the bok choy and mushrooms and garnish with the goji berries, if desired. Serve immediately.

PART

2

Family-Style Dining

In Taiwan, every dinner with friends or family is enjoyed family-style. Whether it's an everyday meal or a big occasion, family-style dining is the way to go in Taiwanese culture. This part of the cookbook features recipes to give you that experience. Family-style is the best way to eat because every dish is meant for sharing; you can try so many dishes from throughout this book—you get all different types of meat, seafood, soup, noodles, and rice—and can customize a meal to serve for your friends and family. There is nothing I love more than having a big feast with my family and friends, and I want to share these fulfilling experiences with you!

小菜
Small Plates

In Taiwan, every family gathering starts with small plates, 開胃菜 kai wei cai, to "open up your appetite." These refreshing appetizers easily pair with any entrée. At almost every restaurant you go to in Taiwan, whether it's big or small, there is a wide selection of appetizers at the front that you can choose from. Because Taiwan is so hot in the summer, people often aren't very hungry come mealtime.

Many of the appetizer recipes in this section can easily be made in bulk and kept in your fridge to enjoy throughout the week. Super convenient!

Pickled Cucumber

花瓜

Huagua

 SERVES 4

1 cup light soy sauce

1 cup rice vinegar

1 cup sugar

15 Persian cucumbers, cut into ½-inch-thick slices

You will find pickled cucumber at street vendors throughout Southern Taiwan. It's the perfect blend of crunchy, sweet, and tangy. Though you can eat it on its own, it's often served with congee. It's so easy to make, and it's one of my favorite ways to use up cucumbers if I have some left in the fridge. The cucumber stays super crunchy, even without any preservatives, and if you don't have anything in the fridge for dinner, you can pair this with rice for a quick, super-yummy, and healthy meal.

1. In a large pot, stir together the light soy sauce, rice vinegar, and sugar. Bring to a simmer over medium heat and simmer for 5 minutes. Add the cucumbers, cover with a lid, and simmer for another 10 minutes.

2. Remove from the heat. Using a spider or metal tongs, transfer the cucumbers to a large bowl, leaving the sauce in the pot. Let the cucumbers sit at room temperature until cool, about 30 minutes.

3. Once the cucumbers are cool, reheat the sauce over medium heat. Return the cucumbers to the sauce and cook for another 5 minutes. This step will ensure that the cucumbers stay crunchy. Remove from the heat and let cool completely in the sauce.

4. Transfer the cucumbers and the sauce to an airtight container and let marinate in the fridge for at least 24 hours before serving. The cucumbers can be stored in the fridge for up to 2 weeks.

家常主菜

Family-Style Entrées

When you walk into a Chinese restaurant, you get handed the world's thickest menu, with seemingly endless options to choose from. You have all kinds of meat, vegetables, seafood, rice, noodles, and soups—practically every single thing you could ever want is in there! Here are some of my favorite large shareable entrées that are easy to make at home. These are the kind of classic Taiwanese large entrée dishes that you typically see at large gatherings, or 請客 ging ke, paired with rice or noodles, or enjoyed on their own. They are so delicious and crowd-pleasing that your friends and family are going to think you ordered from a restaurant. In fact, why not share my cookbook with them like a menu and let them pick and choose what they want to eat!

素食	雞	海鮮	牛	豬
Vegetarian	Chicken	Seafood	Beef	Pork
115	124	132	140	148

Crispy Fried Beans

蒜蓉炒四季豆

Suan rong chao siji dou

 SERVES 4

½ cup canola oil

1 pound / 450g green beans or string beans, ends trimmed

3 tablespoons Garlic Oil (page 246)

½ teaspoon salt

Crispy fried green beans are a staple in many Taiwanese households. One of my favorite restaurants in Taiwan is Din Tai Fung, and this is my version of their famous green beans. I'm not the biggest fan of vegetables, but this dish is so flavorful and refreshing that I can't stop eating it!

The secret ingredient is the garlic oil. The trick for getting crispy beans is to deep-fry them so that their skin crisps up. We have a term in Taiwan, 下油 xai you, which translates to "down in the oil." This technique involves quickly frying food in hot oil, which cooks the food without causing it to become soggy. It helps keep the texture of vegetables and retain their vibrant colors.

1. Heat the canola oil in a large pot over medium-high heat until it reaches 350°F / 180°C on a deep-frying thermometer. Working in batches to prevent overcrowding, add the green beans and fry for 1 minute on each side. Using a spider or slotted spoon, transfer the beans to a plate lined with paper towel to absorb excess oil.

2. Transfer the fried green beans to a large serving plate. Drizzle with the garlic oil and sprinkle with salt. Serve immediately.

Traditional Taiwanese Sticky Rice

台式油飯

Taishi you fan

 SERVES 4

2 cups white glutinous rice

1 cup dried shiitake mushrooms

1 tablespoon olive oil

4 shallots, sliced

¼ cup sliced peeled fresh ginger

½ cup chopped peeled carrot

½ cup raw cashews

3 tablespoons light soy sauce

3 tablespoons vegetarian oyster sauce

3 tablespoons sesame oil

6 lotus leaves (optional)

For garnish

Fried Shallots (page 249)

Fresh cilantro leaves

Every Asian culture has its own way of making sticky rice. It's a dish that can be eaten on any occasion. It's one of those recipes that seems very simple to make, but there are a lot of important steps to making the perfect rice. You don't want it to be too sticky or soggy, but at the same time you want it to be fully cooked.

This is another recipe that was passed down from my grandma. This is a vegetarian version, but you can add any protein you like. I like to add Chinese sausages, dried shrimp, or chicken.

1. Place the glutinous rice in a large bowl and cover with 8 cups of water. Let soak at room temperature for 4 hours or in the fridge, covered, for 8 hours or overnight. Drain and set aside.

2. Place the dried shiitake mushrooms in a medium bowl and cover with 1⅔ cups of water. Let soak for 30 minutes, or until softened. Strain the mushrooms, reserving the soaking liquid. Squeeze the mushrooms dry and cut into thin strips.

3. Heat the olive oil in a large frying pan over medium heat. Add the shallots and ginger and cook, stirring constantly, for 1 to 2 minutes, until fragrant.

4. Add the carrots, cashews, and mushrooms. Increase the heat to medium-high and sauté for 1 to 2 minutes, until the mushrooms start to sweat. Stir in the light soy sauce, vegetarian oyster sauce, and sesame oil. Add the glutinous rice and mix well to ensure all the rice is coated with the sauce.

5. Pour in the reserved mushroom soaking liquid and cook, gently folding the rice until it has soaked up all the sauce, 3 to 5 minutes. Be gentle to prevent breaking the rice.

6. Fill a pot that will fit a bamboo steamer about a third of the way with water. Bring to a boil over high heat.

7. Line the steamer with perforated parchment paper or lotus leaves. Pour the rice into the steamer, and using a chopstick, poke holes in the rice to allow the steam to rise up evenly. Make as many holes as you can to ensure the rice cooks evenly.

8. Place the steamer over the boiling water, cover, and steam the rice for 25 minutes. Remove the steamer from the pot and let the rice sit, covered, for 15 minutes. Transfer the rice to a large serving bowl or individual bowls. Garnish with the fried shallots and cilantro. Serve immediately.

Grandma's Taiwanese Stir-Fry Noodles

炒米粉

Chao mi fen

 SERVES 4

10 ounces / 300g rice vermicelli noodles

1½ teaspoons olive oil

1 pound / 450g white cabbage (1 large cabbage), sliced

1 cup Chinese celery cut in 2-inch lengths

½ cup thinly sliced peeled carrot

1 cup sliced shiitake mushrooms

½ cup sliced fresh black fungus

¼ cup light soy sauce

3 tablespoons vegetarian oyster sauce

1 teaspoon ground white pepper

½ teaspoon sugar

2½ cups water, more if needed

1 tablespoon Shallot Oil (page 249)

1 tablespoon Fried Shallots (page 249)

Fresh cilantro leaves, for garnish

米粉 me fen, also known as vermicelli noodles, are thin noodles made of rice flour and water and are traditional in Taiwanese stir-fry. The noodles are great at soaking in flavors while also not breaking up in the high heat of stir-frying.

If there's one dish my grandma makes better than anyone else, it's her stir-fry noodles. It has the perfect balance of flavors and textures, and it is packed with vegetables. All her friends and relatives request it when they visit her. This is not a dish you normally find at Taiwanese restaurants in North America, and it's even becoming harder to find in Taiwan nowadays.

At first my grandma didn't want to share this recipe with me because it's her secret recipe. But she came around, and now she's excited to share Taiwanese cuisine with the world. I can't wait for you to try this!

1. In a medium bowl, soak the rice vermicelli in cold water to cover for 5 minutes. Drain and set aside.

2. Heat the olive oil in a large frying pan over medium-high heat. Add the cabbage, Chinese celery, carrots, shiitake mushrooms, and black fungus. Sauté for 2 to 3 minutes, until the mushrooms start to sweat.

3. Add the light soy sauce, vegetarian oyster sauce, white pepper, and sugar. Stir well. Pour in the water and bring to a simmer. Add the noodles and, using chopsticks to prevent breaking the noodles, loosen the noodles. Mix to evenly coat the noodles with the sauce.

4. Reduce the heat to low, cover with a lid, and simmer for 15 minutes. If the noodles are still firm, add more water, 1 tablespoon at a time, until the noodles are fully cooked. Uncover, drizzle in the shallot oil, and add the fried shallots. Gently stir. Transfer to a large serving plate and garnish with the cilantro. Serve immediately.

"Stinky" Tofu

臭豆腐

Chou doufu

 SERVES 4

16 ounces / 450g medium-firm tofu, cut into 2-inch cubes

1 tablespoon salt

2 cups water

1½ cups rice flour or cornstarch

1 cup canola oil, for frying

2½ tablespoons vegetarian oyster sauce

2 tablespoons Garlic Oil (page 246)

1½ tablespoons light soy sauce

2 tablespoons sugar

1 teaspoon sesame seeds

1 cup Taiwanese Pickled Cabbage (page 250)

Chopped fresh cilantro leaves, for garnish

It's not a trip to Taiwan without going to the night market and trying stinky tofu! The tofu is traditionally fermented in a brine with vegetables and meats, sometimes for months—hence the "stinky." The strong odor is definitely an acquired taste! I remember walking by these stalls as a kid and thinking, "Who would eat this?" But after I tried it, I grew to love and appreciate the dish. I tried frying it myself at home once, and it was so smelly that I created this version, which uses regular tofu so it's not stinky at all. But it incorporates garlic sauce and cabbage salad, so it still tastes authentic.

Unlike many other fried tofu dishes, stinky tofu is crispy on the outside but juicy on the inside. When you bite into it, you can feel the juices burst into your mouth!

1. **Prepare the tofu:** Place the tofu in a medium bowl and add the salt and water. The tofu should be covered. Let sit for 30 minutes. The brine will draw out excess moisture from the tofu, helping it become extra crispy on the outside but stay juicy on the inside when cooked.

2. Drain the tofu and gently pat dry.

3. Place the rice flour in a large bowl. Add the tofu and lightly toss to coat in the rice flour, being careful not to break up the tofu. Let the tofu sit in the rice flour for 5 minutes.

4. **Fry the tofu:** Heat the canola oil in a large frying pan over medium-high heat until it reaches 325°F / 160°C on a deep-frying thermometer. Add the tofu and fry for 3 minutes per side, until crispy and golden brown. Using a spider or slotted spoon, transfer the tofu to a plate.

5. Increase the heat to high and heat the oil until it reaches 350°F / 180°C. Carefully return the tofu to the pan and fry for another 2 minutes so it becomes extra crispy all over. Carefully remove the pan from the heat and transfer the tofu to a plate lined with paper towel to absorb excess oil.

6. In a small bowl, stir together the vegetarian oyster sauce, garlic oil, light soy sauce, sugar, and sesame seeds.

7. **Assemble the stinky tofu cubes:** Cut a small X in one side of each tofu cube and stuff it with pickled cabbage. Transfer the stuffed tofu to a large serving plate and drizzle with half of the sauce. Garnish with the cilantro. Serve the remaining sauce in a small bowl for dipping.

Garlic Enoki Mushrooms

蒜蓉嫩蒸金針菇

Suan rong nen zheng jinzhengu

 SERVES 4

10 ounces / 285g enoki mushrooms

1 tablespoon unsalted butter

2 tablespoons Garlic Oil (page 246)

1 tablespoon vegetarian oyster sauce

½ teaspoon ground white pepper

1 fresh red Thai chili, chopped (optional)

Chopped scallions, green part only, for garnish

Cooked rice (page 241) or your favorite noodles, for serving

When you go to beer houses in Taiwan, one of the most popular dishes is garlic enoki mushrooms wrapped in foil. Super-soft enoki mushrooms are great at soaking up the spicy, garlicky sauce. This is one of those dishes that is so easy to make. Wrap everything up in foil or parchment paper and pop it in the oven—that's it! This pairs perfectly with a bowl of rice, or you can enjoy it on its own.

1. Preheat the oven to 380°F / 195°C.

2. Place an 8 by 12-inch rectangle of aluminum foil (large enough to wrap the enoki mushrooms) on a work surface. Spray or brush the foil with olive oil to prevent the mushrooms from sticking.

3. Trim away about 1 inch from the root end of the enoki. Place the enoki in the middle of the foil. Top with the butter. Drizzle the garlic oil and vegetarian oyster sauce over the mushrooms and sprinkle with the white pepper and chili, if using. Tightly wrap to prevent any leaking.

4. Place the wrapped enoki mushrooms on a baking sheet and bake for 20 minutes. Let sit until cool enough to handle.

5. Unwrap the foil package. The mushrooms should be soft and the butter should be melted. Mix everything together and transfer to a serving plate. Garnish with the scallions and serve with rice or noodles.

Scallion Chicken

蔥油雞

Cong you ji

SERVES 4

1 (2-inch) piece fresh ginger, peeled and cut lengthwise into 3 slices

2 whole scallions

5 garlic cloves, smashed

1 whole chicken (3 pounds / 1.4kg)

Sauce

2 tablespoons sesame oil

2 tablespoons grated peeled fresh ginger

1 tablespoon grated garlic

3 scallions, chopped, green parts reserved for garnish (optional)

1 teaspoon salt

½ teaspoon ground white pepper

¼ cup vegetable oil

NOTE: Don't throw out the chicken stock! Use it to make soups or to cook rice. Once the stock cools, strain it into an airtight container and store in the freezer for up to 1 month to have chicken stock ready to go. Thaw the stock in the fridge overnight before using.

Scallion chicken is a Taiwanese classic, and you see it at every large family gathering, or qing ke, in Taiwan. Everyone loves it. This is one of those recipes where you really get to taste the ingredients in their purest forms, since there are no intense flavors burying anything. It's so simple yet so yummy. When we first immigrated to Canada, we didn't have a lot of friends, so we weren't invited to many gatherings. However, I was always craving scallion chicken. Before my mom perfected her recipe, we would order takeout, and my mom, sister, and I would just enjoy the scallion chicken on our own with rice over the next few days because it was so satisfying—chicken, rice, and the delicious sauce all in one dish. Fast-forward to today, and this is the recipe my mom makes for me whenever I come back from a long trip abroad.

1. **Cook the chicken:** In a large pot, bring 4 cups of water (enough to cover two-thirds of the chicken), the ginger, whole scallions, and garlic to a rapid boil over high heat.

2. Carefully lower the chicken breast-side up into the pot. The breast should not be covered with water. This way, the breast will steam, staying juicy and tender. Cover with a lid and simmer over medium-high heat for 18 minutes (6 minutes per pound / 450g). To test whether the chicken is cooked, pierce the thickest part of the chicken to make sure the juices run clear. Remove from the heat and let sit with the lid on for another 10 minutes.

3. **Meanwhile, make the sauce:** In a medium heatproof bowl, stir together the sesame oil, ginger, garlic, scallion whites, salt, and white pepper.

4. Heat the vegetable oil in a small saucepan over medium heat until it reaches 225° to 250°F / 110° to 120°C on a deep-frying thermometer. Carefully pour the hot oil into the sauce and stir.

5. Remove the chicken from the stock and transfer, breast-side up, to a large heatproof bowl. Immediately drizzle the hot sauce over the chicken; this will prevent the meat from drying out. Let sit for 10 minutes, until it is safe to touch. (See Note for ways to use the chicken stock.) Transfer the chicken to a cutting board and slice into bite-size pieces. (Reserve the hot sauce.)

6. When ready to serve, transfer the sliced chicken to a large plate. Pour half of the hot sauce all over the chicken. Garnish with the scallion greens, if desired. Serve the remaining sauce on the side for dipping.

Salt and Pepper Chicken Wings

椒鹽雞翅

Jiaoyan jichi

SERVES 4

1½ pounds / 675g chicken wings and/or drumettes

2½ tablespoons rice wine (optional)

2 tablespoons light soy sauce

1 large beaten egg

3 tablespoons cornstarch

1 tablespoon garlic powder

1 tablespoon ground white pepper

1 teaspoon baking powder

¼ cup tapioca starch

2 cups canola oil, for frying

1 tablespoon olive oil

6 garlic cloves, minced

2 scallions, chopped, white and green parts separated

3 fresh red Thai chilies, chopped

Salt and Pepper Seasoning

1 teaspoon chicken powder

1 teaspoon ground white pepper

¾ teaspoon salt

½ teaspoon garlic powder

½ teaspoon ground Sichuan peppercorns

¼ teaspoon chili powder

Fresh cilantro leaves, for garnish

Parents always order salt and pepper chicken wings for the kids at the table, but everyone loves them. Who wouldn't devour crispy fried chicken coated in a delicious seasoning with a light kick? It's so easy to make and is such a shareable dish that it's perfect to bring to potlucks, dinner parties, or game nights. It's guaranteed to be a huge hit. My family goes crazy for these wings—we can easily eat pounds at a time!

1. **Marinate the chicken:** In a large bowl, combine the chicken with the rice wine (if using), light soy sauce, egg, cornstarch, garlic powder, white pepper, and baking powder. Using your hands, massage the chicken to ensure it is evenly coated in the marinade. Cover the bowl and let the chicken marinate at room temperature for 20 minutes.

2. **Meanwhile, prepare the salt and pepper seasoning:** Stir together the chicken powder, white pepper, salt, garlic powder, ground Sichuan peppercorns, and chili powder in a small bowl. Set aside.

3. **Coat the chicken and fry:** Evenly sprinkle the tapioca starch onto a large plate. Take each piece of chicken from the marinade and dredge it through the starch, completely coating both sides. Let sit for 5 minutes in the starch. This will ensure the coating does not fall off during frying.

4. When you are ready to fry the chicken, heat the canola oil in a large pot over medium-high heat until it reaches 350°F / 180°C on a deep-frying thermometer. Working in batches, use metal tongs to transfer the chicken to the hot oil and fry for 6 to 7 minutes, until light golden brown. Using the tongs, transfer the chicken to a large plate.

5. When all the chicken has been fried, increase the heat to high until the oil reaches 380°F / 195°C on a deep-frying thermometer. Working in batches, return the chicken to the hot oil and fry for another 1 to 2 minutes; this will make the chicken extra crispy. Using tongs, remove the chicken from the oil and set aside.

6. Heat the olive oil in a large frying pan over medium heat. Add the garlic, scallion whites, and chilies and cook, stirring frequently, for 1 to 2 minutes, until fragrant.

7. Increase the heat to high. Add the fried chicken, sprinkle evenly with the salt and pepper seasoning, and sauté for 1 minute.

8. Transfer to a large plate and garnish with the scallion greens and cilantro. Serve immediately.

Taiwanese Popcorn Chicken

鹽酥雞

Yan su ji

SERVES 4

1½ pounds / 675g boneless, skin-on chicken thighs, cut into 1-inch cubes

3 tablespoons rice wine (optional)

2½ tablespoons light soy sauce

2 tablespoons minced garlic

1 tablespoon five-spice powder

3½ tablespoons rice flour

1 large egg, beaten

2 cups tapioca starch

2 cups canola oil, for frying

2 cups fresh Thai basil leaves

Spice Mixture

½ teaspoon hot paprika

½ teaspoon five-spice powder

¼ teaspoon garlic powder

¼ teaspoon chili powder

¼ teaspoon ground white pepper

A pinch of salt

Many people are introduced to Taiwanese food through trying popcorn chicken and bubble tea. This combination is the main thing that people will go for at night markets—it's impossible to say no to popcorn chicken because it smells so good! The chicken is crispy on the outside and juicy on the inside and finished with fresh Thai basil that gives it an extra kick.

I don't mean to brag, but my dad, who is a self-proclaimed expert in night market food, says that my popcorn chicken tastes even better than the ones you can get at night markets! Plus, this is a gluten-free recipe. If there's one thing in this cookbook that you *need* to make, it's this dish!

1. **Marinate the chicken:** In a large bowl, combine the chicken with the rice wine (if using), light soy sauce, garlic, and five-spice powder. Massage the chicken until it is well coated. Cover the bowl and let the chicken marinate for 20 minutes at room temperature.

2. **Meanwhile, make the spice mixture:** Stir together the paprika, five-spice powder, garlic powder, chili powder, white pepper, and salt in a small bowl. Set aside.

3. **Coat and fry the chicken:** After 20 minutes, add the rice flour and egg to the chicken mixture. Mix until every piece of chicken is thoroughly coated. You want a wet batter consistency.

4. Add the tapioca starch and toss to coat the chicken well. Let sit for 5 to 7 minutes in the bowl to prevent the coating from falling off during frying.

5. When you are ready to fry the chicken, heat the canola oil in a large pot over medium-high heat until it reaches 350°F / 180°C on a deep-frying thermometer. Add the basil leaves to the hot oil and fry for 30 seconds to 1 minute, until crispy. Using a spider or slotted spoon, remove the basil and set aside on a large plate lined with paper towel to absorb excess oil.

6. Working in batches, carefully place the chicken in the hot oil and fry for 4 to 5 minutes, until golden brown. Using the spider, transfer the chicken to a large plate.

7. When all the chicken has been fried, increase the heat to high until the oil reaches 380°F / 195°C on a deep-frying thermometer. Working in batches, return the fried chicken to the hot oil and fry for 30 seconds. Add the fried basil and fry for another 30 seconds.

8. Transfer to a large plate. Sprinkle with the seasoning mixture. Serve immediately.

Three Cup Chicken

三杯雞

San bei ji

SERVES 4

1½ pounds / 675g chicken wings and/or drumettes

1 tablespoon olive oil

2 (2-inch) pieces fresh ginger, peeled and cut lengthwise into 6 slices each

2 fresh red Thai chilies, chopped

6 garlic cloves, thinly sliced

½ cup rice wine

½ cup light soy sauce

⅓ cup sesame oil

2 tablespoons dark soy sauce

3 tablespoons sugar

1½ cups fresh Thai basil leaves

Cooked rice (page 241) or your favorite noodles, for serving

If you visit Taiwan, you have to check out a 九九快炒店 99 stir-fry store—the Taiwanese version of a beer garden. There are so many yummy dishes, all of them are NT$99 (about US$3.35), and you can enjoy them with beer. Probably the most famous dish at these restaurants is 三杯雞 three cup chicken. The origins of this Taiwanese classic date back to the thirteenth century. While the name "three cup" is thought to stem from using 3 cups each of soy sauce, rice wine, and sesame oil, most recipes call for three *equal parts* of those. You'll typically see this dish served in a clay pot, which helps accentuate the fragrances and flavors. It's popular for a reason, as it is very 下飯 xia fan, which translates to "down rice," meaning you will be downing bowls and bowls of rice with it because of how scrumptious it is! Even though this dish is in the family-style dining section, it's so quick to cook that I make it all the time for weeknight dinners.

1. Bring a large pot of water to a rapid boil over high heat. Add the chicken and blanch for 2 minutes. Drain the chicken, rinse with cold water, then pat dry. The blanching will help remove the impurities from the chicken.

2. Heat the olive oil in a large frying pan over medium-high heat. Add the ginger and sauté for 1 to 2 minutes, until fragrant. Add the chicken, chilies, and garlic. Fry the chicken for 2 to 3 minutes per side, until golden brown.

3. Pour the rice wine, light soy sauce, sesame oil, dark soy sauce, and sugar into the pan. Mix well, cover with a lid, and cook, undisturbed, for 6 minutes, until the mixture has thickened.

4. Increase the heat to high. Add the basil and sauté for another 1 minute.

5. Transfer to a plate and serve with rice or noodles.

Garlic and Scallion Lobster

蔥蒜龍蝦

Cong suan longxia

SERVES 4

4 pounds / 1.8 kg fresh lobster, cut into 3- to 4-inch pieces

2 cups cornstarch

2 cups canola oil, for frying

1 tablespoon olive oil

1 (2-inch) piece fresh ginger, peeled and cut lengthwise into 4 slices

6 scallions, cut into 3-inch lengths, white and green parts separated

¼ cup thinly sliced garlic

2 tablespoons rice wine

3 tablespoons light soy sauce

2 tablespoons sesame oil

1 tablespoon sugar

1½ teaspoons ground white pepper

Cooked rice (page 241) or your favorite noodles, for serving

Garlic lobster is one of those dishes that gets me the most excited whenever I'm going to a wedding or other special occasion in Taiwan. You really get to taste the fresh, natural flavor of the lobster when it's not overwhelmed by heavy condiments. The scallion and garlic complement the lobster beautifully. This recipe is inspired by Yilan, a Taiwanese city that is known for its fresh seafood. I remember going with my dad to restaurants in Yilan where you could select from their catch of the day and they cooked it to your liking based on what was in season. My favorite thing to order was always lobster, and they would always stir-fry it just like this recipe. I promise you are going to love it!

You can ask your fishmonger to cut the lobster into pieces and clean it for you.

1. In a large bowl, lightly coat the lobster pieces with the cornstarch so there is a thin layer over each piece.

2. Heat the canola oil in a large pot over medium-high heat until it reaches 350°F / 180°C on a deep-frying thermometer. Working in batches, add the lobster to the hot oil and fry for 1 minute, or until the lobster turns bright red. Remove with a spider or metal tongs and set aside on a plate.

3. Heat the olive oil in a large deep frying pan over medium-high heat. Add the ginger and scallion whites and sauté for 2 minutes, until fragrant.

4. Add the garlic and fried lobster and sauté for 2 minutes. Pour in the rice wine, cover with a lid, and cook for 2 to 3 minutes, until fragrant.

5. Uncover the pan, increase the heat to high, and add the light soy sauce, sesame oil, sugar, white pepper, and scallion greens. Sauté for another 1 minute.

6. Transfer to a large serving plate and serve with rice or noodles.

Steamed Garlic Prawns with Vermicelli Noodles

蒜蓉蒸蝦米粉

Suan rong zheng xiami fen

SERVES 4

2 ounces / 45g bean vermicelli noodles or mung bean noodles

10 large fresh head-on prawns

4 tablespoons Garlic Oil (page 246), divided

2 tablespoons rice wine

2 tablespoons vegetarian oyster sauce

1½ tablespoons light soy sauce

1½ teaspoons sugar

For garnish

Chopped fresh cilantro leaves

Chopped garlic

Have you ever looked at a dish in a restaurant and thought, "That must be so hard to make at home!" but it turns out it's really easy? Well, this is one of those recipes! It looks and tastes so fancy, yet it's so simple. It's one of the best dishes to make to impress your friends and family. The vermicelli noodles complement the garlic prawns perfectly and soak up all the delicious sauce.

In Asia, seafood is considered a delicacy. At large dinner gatherings, or qing ke, there are always seafood dishes on the table. It's extremely important to have *fresh* seafood in these instances. And because we want to enjoy the freshness and natural umami flavors of the seafood, we don't overwhelm the dishes with condiments and other heavy flavors.

1. In a medium bowl, soak the vermicelli noodles in hot water to cover for 2 minutes. Drain and transfer to a large heatproof bowl. Set aside.

2. To prepare the prawns, pull off the legs and antennae, leaving the tail and head intact. Using a sharp knife, make a shallow cut along the back of each prawn and remove the vein. To butterfly the prawns, use the knife to cut two-thirds of the way through the prawns. Gently split open like a book and lay flat. This will prevent the prawns from curling up during cooking.

3. Lay the prawns cut-side up on top of the noodles in the bowl. Drizzle 2 tablespoons of the garlic oil and the rice wine over the prawns.

4. Fill a steamer pot a third of the way with water and bring to a boil over high heat. Place the bowl with the noodles and prawns on the steamer tier, cover with the lid, and steam for 10 minutes, or until the prawns are bright in color.

5. Meanwhile, in a small bowl, stir together the remaining 2 tablespoons garlic oil, vegetarian oyster sauce, light soy sauce, and sugar.

6. Using a kitchen towel or oven mitts, remove the bowl from the steamer. Drizzle the sauce all over the prawns. Garnish with the cilantro and chopped garlic. Serve immediately.

Spicy Douban Fish with Tofu

麻辣豆瓣魚

Mala douban yu

SERVES 4

1 whole skin-on rockfish or tilapia (1½ pounds / 675g), scaled, washed, and patted dry

4 tablespoons cornstarch, divided

½ cup + 1 tablespoon olive oil, divided

2½ tablespoons la doubanjiang (spicy fermented bean paste)

2 scallions, chopped, white and green parts separated

2½ tablespoons minced garlic

2 tablespoons light soy sauce

1 tablespoon sugar

1½ teaspoons ground Sichuan peppercorns

3 cups chicken stock or vegetable stock

2 cups cubed soft tofu

¼ cup cold water

Cooked rice (page 241) or your favorite noodles, for serving

This is another one of my grandma's secret recipes. The spicy sauce is rich and super delicious—it's made with 辣豆瓣酱 la doubanjiang, or spicy fermented bean paste. This paste is extremely popular in Sichuan cooking and many other regions of China. There are two kinds: spicy bean paste and non-spicy bean paste, also referred to as fermented black bean paste. It's known for its umami flavor and is a staple in my kitchen. This spicy fish with tofu is another dish that is 下飯 xia fan, meaning you will be devouring endless bowls of rice with it!

Any white fish will work for this recipe, such as cod, haddock, or halibut, and if you can't find a whole fish you can just use fillets.

1. On a large plate, dredge the fish in 2 tablespoons of the cornstarch, coating both sides. Let sit on the plate for 5 minutes.

2. Heat ½ cup of the olive oil in a large frying pan over medium-high heat. Lay the fish (skin-side down if using fillets) in the pan and fry for 3 to 4 minutes per side, or until crispy and golden brown. Transfer the fish to a plate. Pour out the oil and wipe the pan.

3. In the same pan, heat the remaining 1 tablespoon olive oil over medium-high heat. Add the doubanjiang, scallion whites, and garlic. Sauté for 2 minutes, until fragrant. Add the light soy sauce, sugar, and ground Sichuan peppercorns and sauté for another 1 minute, until the sugar has dissolved.

4. Pour the chicken stock into the pan and bring to a simmer. Add the fried fish and cook for another 8 minutes, turning halfway through. Add the tofu and simmer for another 3 minutes.

5. In a small measuring cup, stir together the remaining 2 tablespoons cornstarch and the cold water until smooth. Pour the cornstarch mixture into the pan and stir well. Simmer for 1 minute.

6. Transfer to a large serving plate with rice or noodles. Garnish with the scallion greens. Serve immediately.

Garlic Fried Clams

蒜蓉炒蛤蜊

Suan rong chao geli

SERVES 4

1 pound / 450g fresh soft-shell clams, scrubbed

2 tablespoons salt

1½ teaspoons olive oil

1 (2-inch) piece fresh ginger, peeled and julienned

2 tablespoons minced garlic

1 tablespoon chopped fresh red Thai chili

3 tablespoons rice wine

2 tablespoons oyster sauce

1½ teaspoons sugar

Chopped fresh cilantro leaves, for garnish

If you visit a 九九快炒店 99 stir-fry store in Taiwan, you're bound to find garlic clams on offer for NT$99 (about US$3.35). It's one of those dishes that is perfect in summer paired with a glass of ice-cold beer. It's salty, sweet, and spicy all at once. Every time I make this dish, I'm reminded of when my grandpa visited me in Canada a few years ago. My grandpa follows a very strict order when it comes to eating. He always drinks soup first, then eats his vegetables, followed by proteins with rice. He's been doing this his entire life. But when he smelled my garlic clams cooking in the kitchen, he said, "Forget about my rules. Get me a bowl of rice because I'm about to dig in!" I know, like him, you won't be able to resist these garlic fried clams.

1. Soak the clams in a large bowl of cold water with the salt for 30 minutes. This will help release the sand from the clams. Drain.

2. Heat the olive oil in a large frying pan over medium-high heat. Add the ginger, garlic, and chili and sauté for 2 minutes, until fragrant.

3. Add the clams and drizzle in the rice wine, oyster sauce, and sugar. Mix well, cover with a lid, and cook until the clams have opened up, about 5 minutes. Discard any unopened clams.

4. Tip the clams onto a large plate. Garnish with the cilantro and serve immediately.

Scallion Beef Stir-Fry

葱爆牛肉

Cong bao niurou

SERVES 4

1½ pounds / 675g New York strip steak (or your preferred cut of beef)

1½ tablespoons cornstarch

1 teaspoon baking soda

1 large egg white

3 tablespoons rice wine (optional)

A pinch each of salt and ground black pepper

2 tablespoons light soy sauce

1½ tablespoons vegetarian oyster sauce

1 tablespoon sugar

1 teaspoon ground Sichuan peppercorns

1 teaspoon ground cumin

1 cup + 1 tablespoon olive oil, divided

1 cup finely chopped yellow onion

6 scallions, cut into 2-inch lengths, white and green parts separated

10 dried red Thai chilies

Cooked rice (page 241) or your favorite noodles, for serving

Scallion beef stir-fry, or 葱爆牛肉 cong bao niurou, is one of my husband Dom's favorite dishes, as he absolutely loves beef. Beef with onion and scallion is a match made in heaven!

Often, the thing people worry about when cooking beef at home is that the meat is going to turn out chewy and tough. For this recipe, a friend who owns a restaurant in Taiwan shared with me some tricks restaurants use to get tender beef every single time!

1. Place the beef in the freezer for 10 minutes. This will firm up the beef, making it easier to slice. Cut the beef diagonally against the grain into thin strips.

2. In a large bowl, stir together the cornstarch, baking soda, egg white, rice wine (if using), and salt and pepper. Add the beef strips, mix to completely coat the beef, and let marinate for 20 minutes at room temperature.

3. In a small bowl, stir together the light soy sauce, vegetarian oyster sauce, sugar, ground Sichuan peppercorns, and cumin.

4. Heat 1 cup of the olive oil in a large frying pan over medium-high heat. Add the beef strips and fry for 2 to 3 minutes, until browned. Transfer the beef to a plate and set aside. Pour out the oil and wipe the pan.

5. In the same pan, heat the remaining 1 tablespoon olive oil over medium-high heat. Add the yellow onion, scallion whites, and chilies. Sauté for 2 to 3 minutes, until fragrant. Drizzle in the sauce and cook, stirring, for 1 minute.

6. Increase the heat to high. Return the beef to the pan and sauté for 2 minutes. Add the scallion greens and sauté for 30 seconds.

7. Transfer to a large serving plate. Serve with rice or noodles.

Satay Beef Stir-Fry

沙茶牛肉

Shacha niurou

SERVES 4

2 pounds / 900g New York strip steak (or preferred cut of beef)

3 tablespoons rice wine (optional)

1½ tablespoons cornstarch

1 teaspoon baking soda

1 large egg white

A pinch each of salt and ground black pepper

2 tablespoons Taiwanese shacha sauce

2 tablespoons vegetarian oyster sauce

1 tablespoon Chili Oil (page 245) or your favorite brand

1 tablespoon light soy sauce

1 tablespoon minced garlic

1½ teaspoons sugar

½ teaspoon ground black pepper

1 cup olive oil

1 cup finely chopped yellow onion

For garnish

Chopped fresh cilantro leaves

Sesame seeds

If there is one dish that I really came around to loving, it's satay beef stir-fry. Taiwanese shacha sauce (also sometimes spelled sha cha or sacha), or satay sauce, is also known as Chinese BBQ sauce, but it's not anything like North American BBQ sauce. It's also different from the peanut-based satay sauce that is popular in Malaysian and Indonesian cuisine, even though it shares the same name. It is traditionally made from garlic, chilies, shallots, dried shrimp, and Chinese brill, so it has a very intense smell that definitely takes some getting used to. When I was in kindergarten my dad took me to a famous restaurant in Taiwan that specialized in satay, or 沙茶 shacha. I remember walking into the restaurant and being hit with that intense smell. I immediately ran outside and threw up! To this day I find this memory so funny because shacha sauce is now one of my *favorite* condiments. It pairs so perfectly with beef that I even use it on its own as a hot pot dipping sauce. I hope you enjoy this recipe and don't get too scared off by the sauce like I did as a kid.

1.   Place the beef in the freezer for 10 minutes. This will firm up the beef, making it easier to slice. Cut the beef diagonally against the grain into thin strips.

2.   In a large bowl, stir together the rice wine (if using), cornstarch, baking soda, egg white, and salt and pepper. Add the beef strips, mix to completely coat the beef, and let marinate for 20 minutes at room temperature.

3.   In a medium bowl, stir together the shacha sauce, vegetarian oyster sauce, chili oil, light soy sauce, garlic, sugar, and black pepper.

4.   Heat the olive oil in a large frying pan over medium-high heat. Add the beef and fry for 2 to 3 minutes, until browned. Transfer to a large plate.

5.   In the same pan (no need to wipe the pan), over medium-high heat, add the onions and sauté for 3 to 4 minutes, until translucent. Return the beef to the pan and drizzle in the sauce. Increase the heat to high and sauté for 2 minutes.

6.   Transfer to a large plate and garnish with the cilantro and sesame seeds. Serve immediately.

Clear Broth Beef Noodle Soup

清燉牛肉麵

Qingdun niurou mian

SERVES 4

2 star anise pods

1 bay leaf

2 tablespoons white peppercorns

1 tablespoon Sichuan peppercorns

2½ pounds / 1.125 kg beef finger meat, cut into 3-inch pieces

2 pounds / 900g daikon, peeled and cut into 2-inch pieces

1 yellow onion, peeled and cut in half

2 whole scallions

5 cloves garlic, smashed

1 (2-inch) piece fresh ginger

2 tablespoons rice wine

8 cups water

A pinch of salt

2 batches (8 ounces / 225g each) cooked Hand-Cut Noodles (page 242)

For garnish

Fresh cilantro leaves

Chopped scallions, both white and green parts

Chili Oil (page 245) or your favorite brand (optional)

A variation of beef noodle soup, this clear broth beef noodle soup, or 清燉牛肉麵 qingdun niurou main, is definitely an underrated dish. It's not mainstream in the Western world so it's harder to find at Chinese or Taiwanese restaurants in North America. This soup is a personal favorite— I like the clear broth version better than the traditional beef noodle soup. I don't even need the noodles. Just drinking the soup on its own is so good! You really get to taste the herbs, the fragrant beef stock, and how they blend together to make a delicious aromatic soup. Even though it gets really hot in the summer in Taiwan, this is our top choice when we're craving a bowl of noodle soup, because it's not heavy. When you visit restaurants that serve this in Taiwan, there's always a big jar of chili oil on the serving table. I recommend you enjoy a few sips of the clear soup first, then if you want to spice it up you can add some chili oil.

1. In a small frying pan, combine the star anise, bay leaf, white peppercorns, and Sichuan peppercorns. Toast over medium-high heat for 2 to 3 minutes, until fragrant. Transfer the spices to a small plate and let cool. Place the spices in a spice bag.

2. Bring a large pot of water to a rapid boil over high heat. Add the beef and blanch for 3 minutes. Drain the meat and rinse with cold water. This helps remove the impurities from the beef and helps prevent a cloudy broth. Wipe the pot.

3. Return the beef to the pot and add the spice bag, daikon, yellow onion, whole scallions, garlic, ginger, rice wine, and water. Bring to a rapid boil over high heat and cook for 10 minutes. Reduce the heat to low, cover with a lid, and simmer for 1 hour. Check occasionally to ensure the beef is completely covered with water. Add more water as needed.

4. Remove the daikon and beef and then strain the broth before using. Taste and add salt as needed. Discard the spice bag.

5. To assemble, combine the noodles, daikon, and beef in a large bowl. Pour the broth into the bowl. Garnish with the cilantro and chopped scallions. Drizzle with chili oil (if using) or enjoy it on the side as a dipping sauce for the beef. Serve immediately.

Braised Sticky Pork Belly

紅燒五花肉

Hongshao wuhuarou

SERVES 4

1 small cinnamon stick

4 star anise pods

5 fresh red Thai chilies

2½ pounds / 1.125kg pork belly, cut crosswise into 2-inch-thick pieces

1½ teaspoons olive oil

1 (2-inch) piece fresh ginger, peeled and cut lengthwise into 4 slices

10 garlic cloves, peeled and smashed

2 scallions, both white and green parts, cut into 2-inch pieces

4½ tablespoons brown sugar or rock sugar

¼ cup light soy sauce

¼ cup dark soy sauce

3 tablespoons rice wine (optional)

2 cups water

Chopped scallions, green part only, for garnish

Whenever I'm at my grandma's house in Taiwan and I'm hungry, there's always braised pork belly in the fridge. It's so easy to make and is something that truly tastes good with everything. You can put it on top of rice or noodles or inside my gua bao for a Taiwanese pork belly sandwich (page 104). What really makes this dish is doing the prep work correctly—a little love goes a long way!

1. Place the cinnamon stick, star anise, and chilies in a spice bag. Set aside.

2. Bring a large pot of water to a rapid boil over medium-high heat. Add the pork belly and cook for 4 minutes. Drain the meat and rinse with cold water. This will help remove any impurities from the pork belly.

3. Heat the olive oil in a large pot over medium-high heat. Add the pork belly and cook for 2 minutes per side, or until browned.

4. Add the ginger, garlic, and scallions and sauté for 2 minutes, until fragrant.

5. Add the spice bag, brown sugar, light soy sauce, dark soy sauce, rice wine (if using), and water. Increase the heat to high, bring to a rapid boil, and cook for 5 minutes, stirring frequently to prevent the sugar from caramelizing at the bottom of the pot.

6. Reduce the heat to medium-low, cover with a lid, and simmer for 30 minutes, stirring every 5 minutes to ensure everything cooks evenly.

7. Increase the heat to high, remove the lid, and cook for another 5 minutes, or until the sauce is reduced and sticky.

8. Transfer to a large serving plate and garnish with the chopped scallion greens. Serve immediately.

Traditional Beef Noodle Soup

牛肉麵

Niurou mian

SERVES 4

2 star anise pods

6 dried red Thai chilies

2 bay leaves

1 small cinnamon stick

1 tablespoon Sichuan peppercorns

2½ pounds / 1.125kg boneless beef shank, cut crosswise into 3 pieces

1½ teaspoons olive oil

1 cup finely chopped yellow onion

¼ cup smashed peeled garlic cloves

3 thin slices peeled fresh ginger

2 medium tomatoes, sliced ⅛ inch thick

2½ tablespoons la doubanjiang (spicy fermented bean paste)

1½ tablespoons sugar

½ cup rice wine

½ cup light soy sauce

¼ cup dark soy sauce

8 cups water, more as needed

1 batch (8 ounces / 225g) cooked Hand-Cut Noodles (page 242)

4 steamed baby bok choy, cut in half lengthwise

For garnish

½ cup Asian pickled mustard greens

Fresh cilantro leaves

Chopped scallions, green part only

What would a Taiwanese cookbook be without arguably the most famous dish in Taiwanese cuisine? Taiwanese beef noodle soup is the number one dish in our culture. Every single restaurant and household has their own recipe for this dish. It was so fun growing up in Taiwan and going to friends' houses and trying their moms' take on beef noodle soup. I must have tried more than two hundred different versions! Here is my family's recipe. It's slightly spicy, and I recommend pairing it with my fresh Hand-Cut Noodles (page 242). It truly is a pot of love!

1.   In a small frying pan, combine the star anise, chilies, bay leaves, cinnamon stick, and Sichuan peppercorns. Toast over medium-high heat for 2 to 3 minutes, until fragrant. Transfer the spices to a small plate and let cool. Place the spices in a spice bag. (You can skip using a spice bag if you don't have one, but you'll need to strain the broth before serving.)

2.   Bring a large pot of water to a rapid boil over medium-high heat. Add the beef and blanch for 3 minutes, until the scum has floated to the top. Drain the meat and rinse with cold water. This helps remove the impurities from the beef and helps prevent a cloudy broth. Wipe the pot.

3.   In the same pot, heat the olive oil over medium heat. Add the yellow onions, garlic, ginger, and tomatoes and sauté for 3 minutes. Add the doubanjiang and sugar and stir for 1 minute.

4.   Add the rice wine, light soy sauce, dark soy sauce, spice bag, beef, and the water. Ensure the beef is covered with water. Bring to a simmer over low heat, cover with a lid, and simmer for 1½ hours. Check occasionally to ensure that the beef is completely covered with water. Add more water as needed.

5.   Remove the pot from the heat. Transfer the beef to a large cutting board and cut into thin slices. Discard the spice bag or strain the broth.

6.   To assemble, in a large bowl combine the noodles, bok choy, and sliced beef. Pour the broth into the bowl. Garnish with the pickled mustard greens, cilantro, and scallion greens. Serve immediately.

Pork Belly with Garlic Sauce

蒜泥白肉

Suanni bairou

SERVES 4

2½ pounds / 1.125 kg pork belly, cut crosswise into 6-inch pieces

1 (2-inch) piece fresh ginger cut lengthwise into 4 slices

2 scallions, both white and green parts, cut into 2-inch pieces

1 tablespoon Sichuan peppercorns

1½ teaspoons white peppercorns

2 tablespoons rice wine (optional)

3 tablespoons vegetarian oyster sauce

2 tablespoons light soy sauce

2 tablespoons Garlic Oil (page 246)

1½ teaspoons sesame oil

1 tablespoon sugar

1 teaspoon sesame seeds

1 fresh red Thai chili, chopped (optional)

1 English cucumber, julienned

Chopped fresh cilantro leaves, for garnish

If you're a garlic lover, this dish is *made* for you. My husband isn't normally a fan of pork, but whenever I make pork belly with garlic sauce, he goes crazy. The first time I made this for Dom, he ate an entire bucket of rice with it, it was that good! I highly recommend making this dish if you're having guests over, because the majority of the preparation can be done ahead of time and all you have to do before your guests arrive is make the sauce. It's easily shareable and something I always have on my menu whenever I qing ke, or have guests over. I also find that this dish is a great introduction to Asian food for anyone who isn't accustomed to eating it. It's not a mainstream dish, but it's one that almost everyone adores.

1. In a large pot, combine the pork belly, ginger, scallions, Sichuan peppercorns, white peppercorns, and rice wine, if using. Add enough water (about 5 cups) to cover the pork belly by 3 inches. Bring to a rapid boil over medium-high heat. Boil for 15 minutes, then reduce the heat to low, cover with a lid, and simmer for another 10 minutes. Remove from the heat and let sit with the lid on for 20 minutes.

2. Meanwhile, in a small bowl, stir together the vegetarian oyster sauce, light soy sauce, garlic oil, sesame oil, sugar, sesame seeds, and chili, if using.

3. Transfer the pork belly to a cutting board. Cut the pork crosswise into ¼-inch-thick slices. Discard the cooking liquid.

4. To assemble, pile the cucumbers in the middle of a large plate. Arrange the pork belly slices in a circle around the cucumbers, overlapping slightly. Drizzle half of the sauce over the pork belly. Garnish with the cilantro. Serve the remaining sauce in a small bowl on the side for dipping. Serve immediately.

Taiwanese Braised Pork Rice

滷肉飯

Lu rou fan

SERVES 2

2 pounds / 900g pork belly

1 tablespoon olive oil

½ cup rice wine

½ cup light soy sauce

¼ cup dark soy sauce

2 tablespoons sugar

1 tablespoon five-spice powder

½ teaspoon ground white pepper

3 cups water, divided

1 cup Fried Shallots (page 249), plus more for serving

For serving

4 cups cooked rice (page 241)

4 Braised Taiwanese Yolky Eggs (page 98), cut in half lengthwise

Fresh cilantro leaves

Thinly sliced English cucumber

This is the recipe I am the proudest of in this cookbook. It's my 拿手菜 na shou cai, or "specialty dish," a term we use for one's best dish in their repertoire. I'm not trying to boast, but if there's one thing out of the 88 recipes in this cookbook that I *know* you need to try, it's this dish. This is a traditional Taiwanese recipe that has been passed down from my great-grandmother and perfected through the generations. Even in Taiwan nowadays, it's hard to find this flavor, because the number one secret to making a really good bowl 滷肉飯 lu rou fan is love and patience. Hand-cutting the pork is so important because you'll get the perfect ratio of fat, meat, and pork oil. It is worth the effort, and you can really tell the difference in taste and texture.

There's never a gathering at my place where people aren't requesting my braised pork rice. I suggest making it in bulk and freezing some. If you really want to impress your guests, serve my soy-marinated Taiwanese Eggs (page 98) and Garlic Cucumber Salad (page 97) as well and you will have the Taiwanese recipes I'm proudest of in one meal.

1. Use a cleaver or large knife to cut the pork belly crosswise into ¼-inch-thick strips. Make sure that every piece has a little bit of skin, fat, and meat.

2. Heat the olive oil in a large nonstick frying pan over medium-high heat. Add all the pork belly and sauté for 2 to 3 minutes, until the meat is no longer pink.

3. Add the rice wine, light soy sauce, dark soy sauce, sugar, five-spice powder, and white pepper. Stir to combine.

4. Pour in 2 cups of the water and bring to a simmer, then reduce the heat to low, cover with a lid, and simmer for 40 minutes.

5. Add the fried shallots and the remaining 1 cup water, cover with the lid, and simmer for another 30 minutes, until the pork belly can be easily pierced with a fork.

6. To assemble, spoon the pork belly and sauce over rice in a large bowl. Top with braised Taiwanese yolky eggs and garnish with the cilantro, fried shallots, and cucumber.

Taiwanese Cabbage Rolls

台式高麗菜捲

Taishi gaoli cai juan

SERVES 4

2 pounds / 900g Taiwanese cabbage or white cabbage (1 large cabbage)

1½ pounds / 675g ground pork

2 pounds / 900g shiitake mushrooms, roughly chopped into small pieces

1 cup grated peeled carrot

2 tablespoons grated peeled fresh ginger

2 tablespoons minced garlic

3 scallions, both white and green parts, chopped

2 tablespoons light soy sauce

2 tablespoons vegetarian oyster sauce

1 tablespoon sesame oil

1 tablespoon dashi powder

1 tablespoon ground white pepper

1 teaspoon salt

1 cup dashi stock, for serving (optional)

Before I even started writing this cookbook, I knew I had to include my grandma's Taiwanese cabbage rolls. My grandma FaceTimed my mom and showed her step by step how to make her cabbage rolls, and then my mom passed the recipe along to me. It's very healthy, not heavy, and really yummy. Growing up, I remember my cousins and I would line up at the stove with our bowls whenever my grandma made this for us. She would give us each one cabbage roll and we would run back to the living room and enjoy it in front of the TV. I'm truly blessed to be able to share my family's memories and recipes with you, and I hope you enjoy my grandmother's Taiwanese cabbage rolls.

1. **Prepare the cabbage:** Using scissors, poke 2-inch-deep holes around the stem of the cabbage. This will help with peeling the leaves in step 4.

2. Bring a large pot of water to a rapid boil over high heat. Carefully submerge the cabbage stem-side down in the pot and cook for 10 minutes. Remove the cabbage from the pot and let sit while you prepare the filling.

3. **Prepare the filling:** In a large bowl, combine the ground pork, mushrooms, carrot, ginger, garlic, scallions, light soy sauce, vegetarian oyster sauce, sesame oil, dashi powder, white pepper, and salt. Mix in one direction with a gloved hand until fully combined. Mixing in one direction helps prevent the filling from crumbling during cooking.

4. **Assemble the cabbage rolls and cook:** When the cabbage is cool enough to handle, remove about 10 large leaves. They should peel off easily without breaking. Pat dry and lightly score the stems so they won't break when rolled.

5. Working with one cabbage leaf at a time, lay the leaf on a work surface with the stem end facing you. Place about 3 tablespoons of the filling at the bottom of the leaf. Fold in the two sides, then roll up the leaf from the bottom to the top. Repeat with the remaining leaves and filling.

6. Fill a steamer pot about a third of the way with water and bring to a boil over high heat. Place the cabbage rolls seam-side down on the steamer tier, cover with the lid, and steam for 25 minutes, or until the filling is fully cooked and the meat is no longer pink.

7. Remove the cabbage rolls from the steamer and transfer to a large plate. Enjoy on their own or with dashi stock, if desired.

PART

3

Make in Bulk

Prepare these bao, wontons, noodles, and dumplings in bulk. All these recipes are freezer-friendly and will save you tons of time throughout the week. You know how Asian grocery stores have frozen foods sections where you'll see lots of dumplings, buns, and noodles? Think of this as like having your own frozen food section at home!

There's nothing I love more than coming home after a long day and knowing that I can easily have dumplings on the table in just 10 minutes. It's just so convenient!

包子

Bao and Buns

It goes without saying that my cookbook would not be complete without bao and buns. Every weekend when I was young, I loved being in the kitchen while my mom and grandma would spend hours prepping bao and buns in bulk for the week. These recipes may seem intimidating at first, but trust me, practice definitely makes perfect. Here are some of my family's recipes that we have perfected over time. From Gua Bao (page 161) to Vegetable Buns (page 174), there's something for everyone!

Gua Bao

刈包

 MAKES 7 BUNS

2 cups / 280g all-purpose flour

1 tablespoon sugar

1 teaspoon active dry yeast

½ teaspoon salt

½ cup + 2 tablespoons / 150g room-temperature water

1 tablespoon olive oil, plus more for brushing

Often referred to as Taiwanese tacos, gua bao are soft buns traditionally filled with pork belly, pickled mustard greens, and cilantro, though you can really use any protein of your choice. You just have to make sure that these soft and fluffy little buns are thick enough to be able to fully contain the filling inside.

These delicious buns are found in every night market in Taiwan and are super popular. I had so many people asking for this recipe, but I wanted to save it for this cookbook because there are a lot of steps to make it foolproof every time. You can easily double or triple the recipe. (See the step-by-step photos for shaping the dough on page 163.)

1. **Make the dough:** In a large bowl, stir together the flour, sugar, yeast, and salt. Make a well in the center of the flour mixture. Pour the water into the well and mix with a chopstick until a shaggy dough forms. Drizzle in the olive oil and knead the dough in the bowl until it forms a rough ball. Cover the bowl with a kitchen towel and let the dough rest for 10 minutes.

2. **Shape the dough:** After 10 minutes, the dough should be softer and easier to knead. Knead the dough in the bowl until it forms a smooth ball. Turn the dough out onto a floured work surface. Use a rolling pin to roll out the dough into a 12 by 7-inch rectangle. Make sure there are no air bubbles. If there are bubbles, fold the dough in half and keep rolling to press out all the bubbles.

3. Orient the dough with a long side facing you. Roll the dough into a large log (photo 1). Cut the log crosswise into seven equal pieces, each about 1 inch wide by 2 inches long (photo 2). Using your hands, roll each piece into a ball (photo 3).

4. On a floured work surface, working with one piece of dough at a time, roll the dough into a 2½ by 4-inch oval about ½ inch thick (photo 4). Brush olive oil over half the oval, then fold the dough in half to form a clamshell shape (photo 5). Repeat with the remaining dough ovals.

5. Line 2 bamboo steamers with steamer liners or perforated parchment paper. Place 3 or 4 gua bao in each steamer, leaving space between them, as they will expand. Cover with a kitchen towel and let the gua boa rise in a warm place for about 50 minutes, until double in size (photo 6). To check whether the dough is ready, gently press a bun with a finger. If the dough slowly returns back to its original shape, it is ready to steam.

Recipe continues

水餃餛飩

Dumplings and Wontons

If there are two things you can always find in my freezer, it is dumplings and wontons. Trust me when I say that homemade dumplings are so much better than store-bought ones in every way. You can customize them based on your liking, and there are so many different variations on how to prepare them. In Taiwan, you can have dumplings and wontons at any time of the day—whether it's breakfast potstickers or for a late-night snack. They are extremely convenient when made in bulk and frozen, making them an easy meal option in a pinch!

Dumpling Wrappers

水餃皮

Shuijiao pi

 MAKES 30 WRAPPERS

½ teaspoon salt

½ cup + 2 tablespoons / 150g room-temperature water

2 cups / 280g all-purpose flour

I think the wrappers are the most important part of dumplings. When a wrapper isn't properly made, it will break when cooking and water will seep into your dumplings, causing the flavors to escape. And nobody likes dumplings that aren't tasty!

Practice makes perfect when it comes to making these wrappers, but the best part about making dumpling wrappers at home is that it's very affordable and uses simple-to-source ingredients. You can also customize them to your liking. For example, if you prefer dumplings that are a little bit more doughy, you can make your wrappers thicker.

1. In a small measuring cup, stir together the salt and water until the salt is dissolved.

2. Place the flour in a large bowl and pour in the salt water. Use a pair of chopsticks to mix the dough until rough in texture (photo 1). Knead the dough in the bowl until it forms a rough ball. Cover the bowl with a kitchen towel and let the dough rest for 10 minutes.

3. After 10 minutes, the dough should be softer and easier to knead. Using your hands, knead the dough in the bowl until it forms a smooth ball (photo 2). Cover and let rest for another 10 minutes

4. Transfer the dough to a floured work surface. Use a rolling pin to roll out the dough into a 6 by 5-inch rectangle. Cut the dough into thirty 1-inch square pieces, each about 15g (photo 3). Using your hands, roll each piece into a ball.

5. On a floured work surface, roll one ball into a 2-inch circle, keeping the middle of the circle at least ⅛ inch thicker than the edges (photo 4). This helps prevent the wrapper from breaking when wrapping. Transfer to a large plate and cover with plastic wrap to prevent it from drying out. Repeat with the remaining dough.

6. If you are not using the wrappers right away, dust both sides of the wrappers with a generous amount of flour to prevent them from sticking together. Stack the wrappers and wrap tightly with plastic wrap to ensure they do not dry out. Store in the fridge for up to 3 days or in the freezer for 1 month. When ready to use, defrost the wrappers for at least 6 hours or overnight in the fridge.

Folding Dumplings

7. **Boil the dumplings:** Bring a large pot of water to a boil over medium heat. Working in batches, add the dumplings and cook until they start floating, about 5 minutes. Make sure the dumplings are not sticking to the bottom of the pot. Once the dumplings start floating, cook for another 2 minutes. Drain, transfer to a large serving plate and cover with a lid. Repeat with the remaining dumplings. Serve with the dipping sauce. Cooked dumplings can be stored in an airtight container in the fridge for 1 day.

or

Pan-fry the dumplings: Heat a drizzle of olive oil in a large frying pan over medium-high heat. Working in batches, add the dumplings flat-side down. Fry for 1 to 2 minutes, until the bottom is slightly brown. Slowly pour in water until one-third of the dumpling is covered. Cover with the lid and cook until the water is fully evaporated, about 4 minutes. Uncover and fry for 1 minute, or until the bottom is lightly crisped Transfer to a large serving plate and cover with a lid. Repeat with the remaining dumplings. Serve with the dipping sauce. Cooked dumplings can be stored in an airtight container in the fridge for 1 day.

FREEZING INSTRUCTIONS: Place uncooked dumplings on a baking sheet lined with parchment paper, making sure they do not touch. Place in the freezer until frozen, at least 2 hours. Transfer the dumplings to a resealable plastic bag and store in the freezer for up to 1 month. You can cook directly from frozen.

Pork and Chive Dumplings

韭菜豬肉餃子

Jiu cai zhurou jiaozi

MAKES 60 DUMPLINGS

Wrappers

2 batches (60 wrappers) Dumpling Wrappers (page 179)

Filling

1 pound / 450g fresh Chinese chives (jiu cai), finely chopped

2 tablespoons sesame oil

1½ pounds / 675g ground pork or chicken

2 tablespoons vegetarian oyster sauce

2 tablespoons light soy sauce

1 tablespoon grated peeled fresh ginger

1 teaspoon chicken powder

1 teaspoon salt

1 teaspoon ground white pepper

Sauce

2 tablespoons black vinegar

1½ teaspoons Garlic Oil (page 246)

1½ teaspoons Chili Oil (page 245) or your favorite brand

A pinch of toasted sesame seeds

Pork and chive dumplings are basically a love–hate relationship. Love because they are *so delicious*. Hate because you smell like chives for the rest of the day! Chinese chives, or 韭菜 jiu cai, used in this recipe, taste more like garlic than chives and can have a very strong smell, especially when cooked. But that doesn't take away from the taste, in my opinion. To me, this is the number one dumpling flavor: the chives and the pork just pair so well together. It's simply the *best*! (See the step-by-step photos to fold the dumplings on page 181.)

1. **Make the filling:** In a large bowl, stir together the chives and sesame oil. Add the pork or chicken, vegetarian oyster sauce, light soy sauce, ginger, chicken powder, salt, and white pepper. Mix until combined. To test whether the filling is spiced to your liking, microwave a teaspoon of filling in a small microwave-safe container for 1 minute, or until fully cooked. Taste and adjust seasonings if needed.

2. **Fold the dumplings:** Set up a small bowl of water. Holding one wrapper in your palm, spoon 1 tablespoon of the filling onto the center of the wrapper (photo 1). Using your fingers, dab some water around the outer edges of the wrapper to help it stick together when folded. Fold the wrapper in half (photo 2), then using the space between your index finger and your thumbs, squeeze the wrapping together on each side while pushing the filling down, forming a ball in the center (photo 3). Make sure that the edges are tightly sealed (photo 4). Repeat with the remaining wrappers and filling.

3. **Make the sauce:** In a small dipping bowl, stir together the black vinegar, garlic oil, chili oil, and sesame seeds.

4. **Boil the dumplings:** Bring a large pot of water to a boil over medium heat. Working in batches, add the dumplings and cook until they start floating, about 5 minutes. Make sure the dumplings are not sticking to the bottom of the pot. Once the dumplings start floating, cook for another 2 minutes. Drain, transfer to a large serving plate, and cover with a lid. Repeat with the remaining dumplings. Serve with the dipping sauce. Cooked dumplings can be stored in an airtight container in the fridge for 1 day.

or

Pan-fry the dumplings: Heat a drizzle of olive oil in a large frying pan over medium-high heat. Working in batches, add the dumpling flat-side down. Fry for 1 to 2 minutes, until the bottom is slightly brown. Slowly pour in water until one-third of the dumpling is covered. Cover with the lid and cook until the water is fully evaporated, about 4 minutes. Uncover and fry for 1 minute

Recipe continues

until the bottom starts to crisp. Transfer to a large serving plate and cover with a lid. Repeat with the remaining dumplings. Serve with the dipping sauce. Cooked dumplings can be stored in an airtight container in the fridge for 1 day.

FREEZING INSTRUCTIONS: Place uncooked dumplings on a baking sheet lined with parchment paper, making sure they do not touch. Place in the freezer until frozen, at least 2 hours. Transfer the dumplings to a resealable plastic bag and store in the freezer for up to 1 month. You can cook the dumplings directly from frozen.

Vegetarian Dumplings

素水餃

Su shuijiao

 MAKES 60 DUMPLINGS

Wrappers

2 batches (60 wrappers) Dumpling Wrappers (page 179)

Filling

1 large white cabbage (1¼ pounds / 570g), finely grated (about 4 cups)

2 tablespoons salt

1¾ ounces / 50g rice or bean vermicelli noodles

4½ tablespoons sesame oil, divided

1½ tablespoons light soy sauce

2 cups finely chopped shiitake mushrooms

½ cup finely grated peeled carrot

3 scallions, chopped, white and green parts separated

¼ cup finely chopped fresh cilantro leaves

3½ tablespoons vegetarian oyster sauce

1 tablespoon mushroom powder

1 teaspoon ground white pepper

Sauce

2 tablespoons black vinegar

1½ teaspoons Garlic Oil (page 246)

1½ teaspoons Chili Oil (page 245) or your favorite brand

A pinch of toasted sesame seeds

One of my best friends is vegetarian and I love making vegetarian dishes for her. Often, recipes for vegetarian dumplings use meat substitutes, but those vary a lot in texture and flavor by brand, so I find the recipes can be inconsistent. Shiitake mushrooms are a great meat alternative, as they have a meaty texture and umami flavor. I consider myself a meat dumpling connoisseur, but I love how refreshing and delicious this mushroom filling is! Plus, it's a great way to get vegetables in your system.

As always, one of the most important steps is to make sure you draw out all the water from your cabbage. This keeps your dumplings from getting too soggy. You can pan-fry or boil these dumplings. (See the step-by-step photos to fold the dumplings on page 181.)

1. **Make the filling:** In a large bowl, combine the cabbage and salt. Massage the salt into the cabbage, then let rest for 20 minutes. This will help draw out the excess water to ensure the cabbage stays crunchy. Transfer the cabbage to a colander and squeeze out the excess water. Return the cabbage to the bowl and set aside.

2. Meanwhile, in a medium bowl, soak the vermicelli noodles in cold water for 5 minutes. Drain. Use scissors to cut the noodles into 1- to 2-inch pieces. Set aside.

3. In a large frying pan over medium heat, combine 2 tablespoons of the sesame oil, light soy sauce, mushrooms, carrots, and scallion whites and cook, stirring frequently, for 2 to 3 minutes, until the carrots soften.

4. Add the cooked veggies to the cabbage. Add the vermicelli noodles, scallion greens, cilantro, vegetarian oyster sauce, the remaining 2½ tablespoons sesame oil, mushroom powder, and white pepper. Mix well to combine.

5. **Fold the dumplings:** Set up a small bowl of water. Holding one wrapper in your palm, spoon 1 tablespoon of the filling onto the center of the wrapper (photo 1). Using your fingers, dab some water around the outer edges of the wrapper to help it stick together when folded. Fold the wrapper in half (photo 2), then using the space between your index finger and your thumbs, squeeze the wrapping together on each side while pushing the filling down, forming a ball in the center (photo 3). Make sure that the edges are tightly sealed (photo 4). Repeat with the remaining wrappers and filling.

6. **Make the sauce:** In a small dipping bowl, stir together the black vinegar, garlic oil, chili oil, and sesame seeds.

Recipe continues

Shrimp and Pork Wontons

鮮蝦餛飩

Xian xia huntun

MAKES 40 WONTONS

40 wonton wrappers, at room temperature

Filling

1 pound / 450g shrimp, peeled and minced (preferably by hand)

½ pound / 225g ground pork or chicken

1 tablespoon oyster sauce

2½ tablespoons peeled grated fresh ginger

2 tablespoons ground white pepper

1 tablespoon dashi powder or chicken powder

1½ tablespoons sesame oil

1 large egg white

4 scallions, both white and green parts, finely chopped

Wontons with Spicy Sauce (optional)

2 tablespoons black vinegar

1 tablespoon Chili Oil (page 245) or your favorite brand

1 tablespoon light soy sauce

A pinch of toasted sesame seeds

Fresh cilantro leaves, for garnish

Fried Shallots (page 249), for garnish

This is the classic wonton recipe you find in most Chinese restaurants. I love making wontons because there are so many different ways to enjoy them. Whether it be deep-fried wontons, wontons with chili oil, or wonton noodle soup—the possibilities are endless! I always have some wontons in the fridge because I can use them in so many different dishes.

Wontons may look more complicated to wrap than dumplings because there are so many steps in the recipe, but they're actually easier to work with because wonton wrappers close a lot easier. This means that water doesn't usually seep into the wonton as much when cooking and it stays intact, keeping all the delicious flavors inside. The key is just making sure everything is secure when you're wrapping.

1. **Make the filling:** In a large bowl, combine the shrimp, pork or chicken, oyster sauce, ginger, white pepper, dashi powder, sesame oil, egg white, and scallion whites. Mix well. To test whether the filling is spiced to your liking, microwave a teaspoon of filling in a small microwave-safe container for 1 minute, or until fully cooked. Taste and adjust seasonings if needed.

2. **Assemble the wontons:** Set up a small bowl of water. Holding one wrapper in your palm, spoon 1 tablespoon of the filling on the center of the wrapper. Fold the wrapper in half to form a rectangle and press the edges to seal. Fold the edge a quarter of the way down. Dab some water on the two ends, then bring the ends together, pressing them to seal. Repeat with the remaining wrappers and filling. (See photos on page 191.)

For Wontons with Spicy Sauce

1. Bring a large pot of water to a boil over medium-high heat. Once the water is boiling, working in batches, add the wontons. Cook the wontons for 4 to 5 minutes, until they start to float. Once all the wontons have floated up, cook for 1 more minute. Drain the wontons and transfer to a large bowl. Repeat with the remaining wontons.

2. In a small bowl, stir together the black vinegar, chili oil, light soy sauce, and sesame seeds.

3. Pour the sauce over the cooked wontons and toss together. Garnish with the cilantro and fried shallots.

Recipe continues

Wonton Noodle Soup (optional)

4 cups chicken stock or vegetable stock

¼ cup light soy sauce

12 (2-inch) slices peeled fresh ginger

¼ cup Fried Shallots (page 249)

4 teaspoons ground white pepper

Fresh cilantro leaves, for garnish

Chopped scallions, green part only, for garnish

Fried Wontons

3 cups canola oil

Chili Oil (page 245 or your favorite brand) or plum sauce, for serving

For Wonton Noodle Soup

1. Bring a large pot of water to a boil over medium-high heat. Once the water is boiling, add the wontons. Cook the wontons for 4 to 5 minutes, until they start to float. Once all the wontons have floated up, cook for 1 more minute. Drain the wontons and transfer to a large bowl.

2. Meanwhile, in a small saucepan, combine the chicken stock, light soy sauce, and ginger. Bring to a simmer over medium-high heat. Add the fried shallots and white pepper. Simmer for another 1 to 2 minutes, until fragrant.

3. Pour the soup over the cooked wontons. Garnish with the cilantro and scallion greens.

For Fried Wontons

1. Heat the canola oil in a large pot over medium-high heat until it reaches 340°F / 170°C on a deep-frying thermometer. Working in batches, add the wontons and fry for 2 to 3 minutes per side, until crispy and golden brown. Transfer to a plate lined with paper towel to absorb excess oil.

2. Serve with chili oil or plum sauce.

FREEZING INSTRUCTIONS: Place uncooked wontons on a baking sheet lined with parchment paper, making sure they do not touch. Place in the freezer until frozen, at least 2 hours. Transfer the wontons to a resealable plastic bag and store in the freezer for up to 1 month.

Shrimp and Pork Wontons (Wontons with Spicy Sauce)

Shrimp and Pork Wontons (Wonton Noodle Soup)

Taiwanese Savory Rice Balls

Yan tang yuan

MAKES 15 RICE BALLS

Dough

2 cups / 200g glutinous rice flour

2 tablespoons sugar

¼ cup hot water

⅓ cup cold water

Filling

1 tablespoon dried shrimp (optional)

7 ounces / 200g ground pork

1 cup finely chopped shiitake mushrooms

1 tablespoon Fried Shallots (page 249)

3 scallions, both white and green parts, finely chopped

2 tablespoons light soy sauce

2 tablespoons vegetarian oyster sauce

1 teaspoon dashi powder

1 teaspoon ground white pepper

Broth

2 cups chicken stock or vegetable stock

1 tablespoon light soy sauce

1 (2-inch) piece fresh ginger, peeled and sliced lengthwise into 3 pieces

1 tablespoon Fried Shallots (page 249)

1 teaspoon ground white pepper

For garnish

Fresh cilantro leaves

Chopped scallions, green part only

Tang yuan is a traditional food that symbolizes togetherness. This dish is typically served sweet and eaten during Lunar New Year. While this savory version is not a mainstream dish, it's still very popular in Taiwan. It contains a flavorful pork filling inside a wrapping that has a soft mochi-like texture. This dish is gluten-free, so it's a great alternative for those who can't eat gluten but want something similar to dumplings.

Food is such a big part of our culture in Asia, and this dish is affordable to make, serves a lot of people, and is delicious at the same time. During election campaigns in Taiwan, many politicians will serve xian tang yuan, savory rice balls, at their campaign speeches. One of my first memories of eating xian tang yuan was during an election. As a child who didn't understand anything about politics, I'd get excited to go down to these events with my parents and get to eat xian tang yuan.

1. **Make the dough:** In a large bowl, mix together the rice flour and sugar. Pour in the hot water and mix with a pair of chopsticks until combined. Slowly pour in the cold water and mix again with the chopsticks. Once the dough is cool enough to handle, use your hands to knead it into a rough ball. Cover the bowl with a kitchen towel and let the dough rest for 15 minutes.

2. **Meanwhile, make the filling:** Soak the dried shrimp (if using) in a small bowl of water for 10 minutes. Drain, pat dry, and finely chop.

3. In a large bowl, combine the dried shrimp, ground pork, mushrooms, fried shallots, scallions, light soy sauce, vegetarian oyster sauce, dashi powder, and white pepper. Mix well.

4. **Shape the rice balls:** Tip the dough onto a floured work surface. Roll out the dough into a long 15-inch log about 1 inch thick with your hands. Cut into fifteen equal pieces. Cover the dough with a damp kitchen towel.

5. Take one piece of dough, leaving the rest covered with the towel. Roll the dough into a ball with the palm of your hand, then use your thumb to make a dent in the center. Place 1 tablespoon of the filling in the dent. Push the filling down with your thumb while gently pinching the top closed. Using your palms again, roll the dough into a smooth ball, making sure the filling is fully enclosed. Repeat with the remaining dough and filling.

6. **Cook the rice balls:** Bring a large pot of water to a boil over high heat. Working in batches, add the rice balls and cook for 10 minutes, or until they start to float. Once all the rice balls are floating, cook for another 2 minutes. Drain the rice balls and transfer to a large bowl. Repeat with the remaining rice balls. Wipe the pot.

Recipe continues

7. **Make the broth and finish:** In the same pot, combine the chicken stock, light soy sauce, and ginger. Bring to a simmer over medium-high heat. Once the broth is simmering, add the fried shallots and white pepper. Simmer for another 1 to 2 minutes, until fragrant. Pour the broth over the rice balls. Garnish with the cilantro and chopped scallion greens.

FREEZING INSTRUCTIONS: Place the uncooked rice balls on a baking sheet lined with parchment paper, making sure they do not touch. Place in the freezer until frozen, at least 2 hours. Transfer the rice balls to a resealable plastic bag and store in the freezer for up to 1 month. You can cook the rice balls directly from frozen.

烘焙
The Ultimate Bakery

In this section, you will find some of my favorite Taiwanese classics. These staple dishes are some of the first things I eat whenever I visit Taiwan. These recipes are more complicated than many in the book, but don't be intimidated! I always say there's no right or wrong when it comes to cooking, and practice really does make perfect. I've included step-by-step photos for each dish, to help you make some of my childhood favorites in your own home. Trust me, you will be so glad you made the effort!

Shao Bing

燒餅

Baked sesame flatbreads

 MAKES 8 FLATBREADS

Dough

2 cups / 280g all-purpose flour, plus
2 tablespoons for dusting

½ teaspoon salt

⅓ cup / 80g hot water

½ cup / 120g room-temperature water

1 tablespoon vegetable oil

Flaky Paste

⅓ cup / 80g all-purpose flour

⅓ cup / 60g vegetable oil

1 cup raw sesame seeds, for coating

燒餅 shao bing, also known as sesame flatbread, is a baked layered flatbread that can be served plain or stuffed, sweet or salty. It's a very popular breakfast pastry in Asia, though it can be hard to find in Western countries. It's not as hard to make as you might think, but there are a few tips that will help you make it just like the street vendors do in Taiwan. You want your shao bing to be crispy on the outside, but puffy and with lots of layers on the inside. The sesame seeds on top become super fragrant while it's baking, and it's one of the most irresistible smells in the kitchen.

You can wrap eggs or any fillings you'd like in shao bing. A popular pairing is you tiao Chinese doughnuts (see my recipe on page 207).

1. **Make the dough:** In a large bowl, stir together the 2 cups of flour and salt. Slowly pour in the hot water while mixing with a pair of chopsticks until it forms a rough texture. Pour in the room-temperature water and vegetable oil and mix again with the chopsticks. Let sit until cool enough to handle.

2. Knead the dough in the bowl into a ball. The dough will be sticky but should be able to peel off the sides of the bowl. If the dough is too sticky to knead, cover with a kitchen towel and let rest for 10 minutes before kneading. Cover the bowl with a kitchen towel and let the dough rest for 30 minutes.

3. **Meanwhile, make the flaky paste:** In a small saucepan, combine the flour and vegetable oil. Stir until smooth. Cook over medium-low heat, stirring constantly, for 3 minutes, or until fragrant. Remove from the heat and let cool.

4. **Roll and shape the dough:** Lightly oil a work surface with a drizzle of vegetable oil and rub some on a rolling pin. Place the dough on the oiled work surface. Use the rolling pin to roll out the dough into an 18 by 10-inch rectangle. Using your fingers, evenly spread about 1½ teaspoons of the flaky paste all over the surface of the dough leaving a ¼-inch border at the bottom edge. Evenly dust the dough with 2 tablespoons of flour.

5. Orient the dough with a long side facing you. Tightly roll the dough down from top to bottom into a log. Make sure that there are no air bubbles (prick any with a toothpick) and that the paste is tucked inside. Cover with a damp kitchen towel and let the dough rest for 20 minutes.

6. Preheat the oven to 450°F / 230°C. Line a large baking sheet with parchment paper.

Recipe continues

Easy Red Bean Soup with Mochi Balls

小湯圓紅豆湯

Xiao tangyuan hongdou tang

 SERVES 3 TO 4

Red Bean Soup

1 cup dried red beans (adzuki beans)

¼ cup purple rice (also known as black rice)

10 cups water (not including water for soaking)

1 cup loosely packed brown sugar

Mochi Balls

1 cup / 100g mochiko (sweet rice flour)

¼ cup / 32g granulated sugar

⅛ cup / 30g hot water

2 tablespoons + 2 teaspoons / 40g room-temperature water

NOTE: These mochi balls can be made in bulk and stored in the freezer for up to 2 months.

The opposite of cold green bean soup (page 216), hot red bean soup is often enjoyed in the winter to "cleanse" the body of cold. This is another recipe that my grandma swears by to help balance the body's systems. Red beans, also known as adzuki beans, are said to replenish blood qi, or energy. Because of red beans' strengthening qualities and high iron content, this soup is ideal to drink during the menstrual cycle and it really helps with cramps. You can also serve this dish cold in the summertime. My favorite way to enjoy this delicious soup is with chewy, soft mochi balls on top.

1. **Soak the red beans and rice:** In a large bowl, combine the red beans and purple rice. Cover with 8 cups of room-temperature water and let soak for 4 hours. Drain. Return the beans and rice to the bowl.

2. **Make the soup:** In a large pot, bring the 10 cups of water to a boil over high heat. Add the drained beans and rice and cook, stirring constantly, for 15 minutes. Reduce the heat to low, cover with a lid, and cook for another 35 minutes, stirring every 10 minutes to prevent the beans and rice from sticking to the bottom of the pot. When the soup is thick and the red beans are soft and slightly opened, add the brown sugar and stir well., Remove the pot from the heat and let sit with the lid on for 20 minutes.

3. **Meanwhile, make the mochi balls:** In a large bowl, stir together the mochiko and granulated sugar. Slowly pour in the hot water, mixing with a pair of chopsticks until flaky. Pour in the room-temperature water and mix again with the chopsticks until the dough is cool enough to touch.

4. Knead the dough in the bowl until it forms a smooth ball.

5. Line a large baking sheet with parchment paper. Roll out the dough into a long rope on a floured work surface with your hands. Cut into ½-inch pieces. Using your hands, roll the pieces of dough into balls. You should have about 20 balls. Place the balls on the prepared baking sheet and place in the freezer for 2 hours, or until hardened. At this stage you can transfer the frozen mochi balls to a resealable plastic bag and store in the freezer for up to 2 months. Cook from frozen as instructed in step 6.

6. Bring a medium pot of water to a rapid boil over medium-high heat. Add all the mochi balls and cook until they start to float, about 15 minutes, stirring every 3 minutes to prevent the balls from sticking to the bottom of the pot. Drain.

7. **Assemble the soup:** Ladle the red bean soup into bowls and top with cooked mochi balls. You can also enjoy the soup cooled in the fridge or add ice cubes.

Taiwanese Sesame and Peanut Mochi

芝麻花生麻糬

Zhima huasheng mashu

 SERVES 2

Mochi

1 cup mochiko (sweet rice flour)

3 tablespoons sugar

1 cup water

Dipping Powder

½ cup ground unsalted peanuts

½ cup sugar, divided

½ cup ground black sesame seeds

When I was growing up in Taiwan, there was a street stall that occasionally set up shop below our apartment that made the *best* Taiwanese mochi. From our bedroom windows, we could see the vendor setting up his stall and we would run downstairs to buy some mochi.

Unfortunately, it's not easy to find traditional mochi in Western countries—especially not freshly made mochi. That's why I want to share with you this recipe that's inspired by my neighborhood street vendor's mochi. This delicious gluten-free snack takes me right back to my childhood.

1. **Make the mochi:** In a large microwave-safe bowl, stir together the mochiko and sugar. Add the water and whisk until there are no lumps. Cover with a microwave-safe plate and microwave on high for 3 minutes.

2. Stir the mixture with a wooden spatula. The mixture will be thick and sticky.

3. Cover again and microwave for another 3 minutes. Again, stir with the wooden spatula. Repeat this process until the mochi mixture is translucent and stretchy. Let sit until cool enough to handle.

4. Use your hands to break off bite-size pieces and roll them into smooth balls, transferring them to a serving plate as you work.

5. **Set up the dipping powder and coat the mochi:** In a medium bowl, stir together the ground peanuts and ¼ cup of the sugar. In a separate medium bowl, stir together the ground black sesame seeds and the remaining ¼ cup sugar.

6. Roll the mochi in the coating of your choice, and serve. The mochi are best enjoyed right away; they will harden if stored overnight.

Almond Cookies

杏仁餅乾

Xingren bingqian

 MAKES 12 COOKIES

2 large egg whites

⅓ cup sugar

A pinch of salt

2 tablespoons + 2 teaspoons / 40g cake flour, sifted

1 cup sliced blanched almonds

2 tablespoons unsalted butter, melted

Thin and crisp almond cookies are the best afternoon snack or dessert. They are not too sweet and are so easy to make. I wrapped these up and gave them to my husband Dom as a Christmas gift on our second date. I'm not sure if it's nostalgia, but to this day Dom says these are the best cookies he's ever had. Almond cookies are often thicker and denser, but I prefer these thin almond cookies because they are so crispy and light.

These super addictive cookies are relatively healthy. The trick to achieving the perfect brittleness and crispness is to spread the batter very thinly onto the baking sheet.

1. In a medium bowl, whisk together the egg whites, sugar, and salt until smooth. Whisk in the cake flour.

2. Gently fold in the almonds. Pour in the melted butter and gently mix until combined. Make sure the almonds are well coated with the mixture. Cover the bowl with plastic wrap and let rest in the fridge for 30 minutes. This allows the gluten in the batter to relax, creating more leavened and crispy cookies.

3. Meanwhile, preheat the oven to 300°F / 150°C. Line a large baking sheet with parchment paper.

4. Scoop 2 tablespoons of the batter onto the prepared baking sheet. Use the back of the spoon to spread the batter into 2-inch circles so the almond slices are evenly spaced and not stacked on top of one another. This helps the cookies to cook evenly and stay thin and crispy. Repeat with the remaining batter. If the batter starts to gather on the spoon, rinse the spoon with water between scoops.

5. Bake for 15 minutes. Carefully turn the cookies over and bake for another 10 minutes, or until golden brown on the top and bottom.

6. Let the cookies cool on the baking sheet for 5 minutes before serving or transfer to racks to cool completely. Store the cookies in an airtight container at room temperature for up to 2 weeks or in the freezer for up to 2 months. If frozen, allow the cookies to defrost at room temperature before serving.

Honey Cake

古早味蛋糕

Gu zao wei dangao

 SERVES 4

4 large eggs

⅓ cup / 80g 2% milk

¼ cup / 57g unsalted butter, cut into
½-inch cubes

½ cup / 70g cake flour

1 tablespoon liquid honey

1 teaspoon pure vanilla extract

⅓ cup / 65g sugar

In Taiwan, our schools used to give us slices of honey cake as the dessert in our lunches. This cake is perfect because it's packed with honey flavor but not too sweet. The texture is like the softest sponge cake, so light and fluffy, and it is one of my favorite treats after a meal. Every bite takes me back to my childhood.

It took my mom and me at least fifty tries to come up with this perfect recipe, so I know it is foolproof. Like any dessert, practice makes perfect. The key to the spongy, soft texture is the combination of baking and steaming. I can't wait for you to try it!

1. Preheat the oven to 300°F / 150°C. Line the bottom and sides of a 6-inch square baking pan with parchment paper, leaving extra overhang on the sides to make it easier to remove the cake.

2. Separate the eggs, placing the yolks in a small bowl and the whites in a very clean large bowl. Make sure there is no egg yolk in the egg whites, or the whites will not whip up properly.

3. Heat the milk and butter in a small saucepan over low heat, slowly stirring until the butter melts. Remove from the heat.

4. Sift the cake flour into a separate large bowl. Slowly pour in the milk mixture while gently stirring in one direction. Once everything is combined, add the egg yolks, one at a time, mixing after each addition until combined. Stir in the honey and vanilla.

5. Using a hand mixer, beat the egg whites until bubbles start to form. While beating, slowly add the sugar, a couple of tablespoons at a time. Keep beating for about 10 minutes, until the egg whites form stiff peaks.

6. Gently fold half of the egg whites into the batter until fully mixed. Add the remaining egg whites and gently fold again. Do not overmix or you will deflate the whites.

7. Pour the batter into the prepared baking pan. Tap the pan on the counter to release any large air bubbles and to level the cake.

8. Place the baking pan in a larger pan. Pour hot water into the large pan until it reaches three-quarters of the way up the side of the baking pan. Bake for 60 minutes until the top is golden brown. Do not open the oven while baking or the cake will deflate.

9. Remove the pan from the water and let the cake cool for 10 minutes before serving. Store in an airtight container at room temperature for up to 3 days.

飲料

Drinks

One of the best things about traveling in Taiwan is that beverages are so popular everywhere you go. When you walk down any street, it seems everyone has some street food in one hand and some form of drink in the other! As well, there are so many different options for beverages. Here are some of my family's drink recipes that are inspired by our beautiful country's popular beverages.

Brown Sugar Milk Tea with Homemade Boba Pearls

紅糖珍珠奶茶

Hongtang zhenzhu naicha

 SERVES 2

Boba Pearls

1¼ cups / 150g tapioca starch, plus ½ cup for rolling

⅓ cup / 80g water

¼ cup / 50g loosely packed brown sugar

Brown Sugar Glaze

½ cup loosely packed brown sugar

Milk Tea

2 cups 1% or 2% milk

4 Taiwanese red tea bags

Ice cubes, for serving

What is a Taiwanese cookbook without the most famous Taiwanese drink of all? Originating in Taiwan in the 1980s, bubble tea, or boba, has since taken the world by storm, with shops popping up everywhere. What makes this drink special is the chewy and sweet tapioca pearls. If you're obsessed with bubble tea like I am, you know that it can get pricey. Save your money and make it at home! If you make boba pearls in bulk, you can have bubble tea at home any time you want!

This recipe is for pearls with a classic brown sugar milk tea, but you can add the pearls to any drink or smoothie you enjoy. Boba pearls are also gluten-free! (See the step-by-step photos to make the boba pearls on page 231.)

1. **Make the boba pearls:** Place the 1¼ cups tapioca starch in a large heatproof bowl.

2. In a small saucepan, combine the water and brown sugar. Heat over medium heat, stirring occasionally, until the sugar is dissolved. Pour the mixture over the tapioca starch and stir quickly with a pair of chopsticks. The dough will be very sticky (photo 1). Let sit until cool enough to handle.

3. Knead the dough in the bowl until it forms a smooth ball (photo 2). Cover with a damp kitchen towel and let sit for 15 minutes.

4. Transfer the dough to a floured work surface. Cut into four equal portions. Working with one portion at a time, roll the dough into a ¼-inch-thick rope (photo 3). Cut the rope crosswise into ¼-inch pieces (photo 4). You can adjust the size depending on how big you prefer your pearls to be. The pearls will expand when cooked.

5. Put about ½ cup of tapioca starch in a medium bowl. Using your hands, roll each piece of dough into a ball and place in the starch (photo 5). Coat the balls with the tapioca starch to prevent them from sticking to each other (photo 6). At this stage you can freeze the balls in an airtight container for up to 1 month.

6. Bring a large pot of water to a simmer over medium heat. Add the tapioca balls and cook, uncovered, for 40 minutes, stirring occasionally so they don't stick to the bottom or sides of the pot. Remove the pot from the heat, cover with a lid, and let sit for 30 minutes. (If you prefer softer pearls, cook for 45 minutes and let rest for 35 minutes.)

7. Drain the pearls. Transfer to a medium bowl of cold water and let sit until you are ready to serve, up to 2 hours.

Recipe continues

8. **When ready to serve, make the brown sugar glaze:** Drain the tapioca pearls. Sprinkle the brown sugar into a large pot. Stir over medium heat for 2 to 3 minutes, until the sugar starts to dissolve, making sure the sugar doesn't burn. Add the boba pearls and stir for another 2 to 3 minutes, until the glaze is thick and every pearl is completely coated. Remove from the heat.

9. **Make the milk tea:** Heat the milk in a medium saucepan over medium heat. Once the milk starts to simmer, add the tea bags and gently stir for 2 to 3 minutes, depending how strong you like your milk tea. Remove from the heat. Discard the tea bags and let the milk cool for 10 minutes.

10. **Assemble the boba milk tea:** Spoon about ¼ cup of boba pearls into each of two large glasses. Fill with ice cubes, then add the milk tea. Serve with a wide straw.

常備品

Back to Basics

Here are some items that are always in my fridge or pantry. Many of them are staples that really elevate any dish. With these basics you can make restaurant-quality meals quickly and easily.

Rice

飯

Fan

SERVES 3 TO 4

2 cups short-grain rice, basmati rice, sushi rice, or brown rice (see Note)

3 cups room-temperature water (see Note)

1 teaspoon olive oil

If there's one simple dish that I can't live without, it's rice. My grandma's nickname for me growing up—because I love rice so much—was 飯桶 fan tong, which literally translates to "rice bucket" but means "rice queen." To this day, I can eat rice with anything. Including goldfish crackers. Yes, you read that right. That's how much I love rice.

Rice may seem like a very basic dish, but perfect rice isn't easy to make. You want to make sure it's the right degree of fluffy, while not being too soggy or sticky. For my day-to-day cooking, I swear by my trusty electric rice cooker. But I understand that not everyone wants to invest in one. So here is my stovetop version that is so easy that anyone can make perfect rice! When I'm traveling and far away from my rice cooker, I use this recipe.

1. In a medium bowl, rinse the rice with water, draining it between rinses until the water is no longer cloudy. This usually takes three or four rinses. Drain.

2. Transfer the rice to a medium pot. Pour in the water and olive oil. You want the water to be about 1 inch above the rice, so don't use a pot that's too big.

3. Cover with a lid and bring to a simmer over medium-high heat. Simmer for 10 minutes. Reduce the heat to low and continue simmering for another 5 minutes. Remove the pot from the heat and let the rice sit, with the lid on, for another 10 minutes.

4. Use a fork to fluff the rice. Scoop the rice into individual bowls or a large serving bowl and serve.

NOTE: An easy way to check whether you have enough water is to measure it with your finger. Rest your index finger on top of the rice. You want the water to reach the first joint of your finger. If using brown rice, soak it in room-temperature water for 2 hours before cooking.

Hand-Cut Noodles

手切麵

Shou qiemian

**SERVES 2
(MAKES 8 OUNCES / 225G)**

½ cup + 2 tablespoons / 150g water

1 teaspoon salt

2 cups / 280g all-purpose flour

One of the questions I'm most frequently asked is what kind of noodles do I use in my recipes. My answer is always "fresh noodles"! Not everyone has access to fresh noodles at their local Asian grocery store, so here's my super-easy recipe. Make noodles in bulk and store in your freezer for months. You can adjust this recipe based on your preference for the thickness of the noodles. These hand-cut noodles can be used in any of the noodle recipes in this cookbook.

1. In a measuring cup, stir together the water and salt until the salt is dissolved.

2. Place the flour in a large bowl. Pour in the salted water and stir with a pair of chopsticks until flaky. Knead the dough in the bowl into a ball. Cover the bowl with a kitchen towel and let the dough rest for 10 minutes.

3. After 10 minutes, the dough should be much softer and easy to work with. Knead the dough in the bowl until it forms a smooth ball. Cover and let rest for another 10 minutes.

4. Lightly flour a work surface and a rolling pin. Place the dough on the work surface and use the rolling pin to roll it out into a 7 by 4-inch rectangle (photo 1).

5. Dust more flour over the rolling pin and roll out the dough until ⅛ inch thick (or your desired thickness).

6. Loosely roll up the dough along the long edge (photo 2). Cut the dough into ¼-inch-wide noodles (photos 3 and 4). If you prefer thicker-cut noodles, cut into wider strips.

7. If not using immediately, store the noodles in individual portions in a resealable plastic bag in the freezer for up to 1 month.

8. When ready to cook the noodles, bring a medium pot of water to a rapid boil over medium-high heat. Add the noodles and cook, stirring occasionally, until they start to float, or until they are your desired texture, 4 to 5 minutes.

Index